Public Speaking Made Simple

Curt Simmons

Edited and prepared for publication by New England Publishing Associates, Inc.

A Made Simple Book

DOUBLEDAY   New York London Toronto Sydney Auckland

Edited and prepared for
publication by New England Publishing Associates, Inc.
Copy Editor and Indexer: Roberta J. Buland
Editorial Administration: David Voytek
Page Composition: Phanyada Sriranpong

A MADE SIMPLE BOOK
PUBLISHED BY DOUBLEDAY
a division of Bantam Doubleday Dell Publishing Group, Inc.
1540 Broadway, New York, New York 10036

MADE SIMPLE and DOUBLEDAY are trademarks of Doubleday,
a division of Bantam Doubleday Dell Publishing Group, Inc.

Library of Congress Cataloging-in-Publication Data
Simmons, Curt
       Public speaking made simple / Curt Simmons: Edited and prepared for
           publication by New England Publishing Associates, Inc.
       p.   cm.
       "A Made Simple Book"
       Includes bibliographical references and index.
       ISBN 0-385-48185-3
       1. Public Speaking
       I. New England Publishing Associates.   II. Title
PN4121.S466   1996
808.5'1--dc20
                                         95-5113
                                         CIP

ACKNOWLEDGEMENTS

I would like to offer a sincere thank you to Curt Beckham, Erica Smith, Duane Choate, and Beth Stokes — my friends and former students who helped edit and verify research information contained in this book. I also owe a special thanks to my parents, Norman and Diane Simmons, who made it possible for me to begin competing in public speaking contests when I was young. Most of all, thanks to my wife, Stacey — my constant source of love, support, and encouragement.

For information about public speaking training workshops for your business or organization, write to Curt Simmons at P.O. Box 633434, Nacogdoches, Texas 75963.

ABOUT THE AUTHOR

Curt Simmons began presenting speeches in high school after he reluctantly entered a contest — and won! Since that time, he has given hundreds of speeches and presentations on various issues and won numerous speaking awards. He holds bachelor's and master's degrees from Stephen F. Austin State University and presently teaches secondary public speaking and English courses. He lives in Nacogdoches, Texas with his wife, Stacey.

CONTENTS

CHAPTER ONE

What Is a Speech?

A name is announced, the audience applauds, and one lone person approaches the front of the room. The crowd stares at this person, makes judgments about his or her appearance, and holds its breath in anticipation. The person begins to speak and, within one minute, the audience members decide whether they like the person and if they will listen to the speech.

This scenario is familiar to us all, and that person walking to the front will soon be you! Like thousands of other people who suddenly find themselves preparing for a speech, you may feel a sense of excitement, fear, and confusion. This book will guide you through these feelings, help you write your speech or presentation, and give you a working list of skills to make your "big day" a success. Whether this is your first speech or if you simply need to polish your skills,

this book will give you the edge you need.

The best way to learn a sport or any new skill is to have a coach or a trainer. Think of this book as your personal speech coach. Follow the instructions and read the chapters in the order they are presented. Often, I will ask you to stop and work on part of your speech. This is the best approach. Once you have finished the book, you will have an effective speech and effective speaking skills. Work on your speech with a note pad or a spiral notebook at hand. This way, all of your work will stay in one place, and you will be able to refer to different sections. With all of that said, we're ready to get started.

First of all, let's examine the differences between a speech and a presentation. A speech is generally considered a formal communication event designed primarily to inform, persuade, or entertain people.

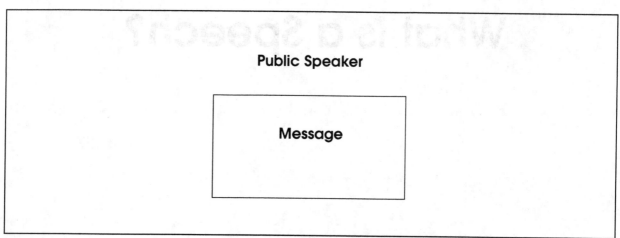

Figure 1. *Communication begins with someone who wants to send a message.*

Speeches are usually given at banquets, formal meetings, dinners, and other formal events. A presentation is usually less formal and concentrates on teaching something to the audience. Some common examples are classes, business meetings, committees, or other specific groups. For our purpose, I will refer to a "speech" as any type of speech or presentation, and the skills we will work on apply to both of these situations.

Before we begin to work on your speech, let's take a look at some basic information about communication. This section will help you understand your purpose as a speaker and the purpose of your speech.

What Is Communication?

Communication can be defined as any act of sending an understandable message to another person or persons. We all communicate every day. In fact, communication is what we spend most of our time doing. The simple test for all types of communication is whether or not the message is understood. Whether you are speaking about travel experiences or nuclear energy, the message must be understood by the audience — or it isn't communication.

There are two basic ways we communicate: verbally, which is spoken language, and nonverbally, which includes gestures, facial expressions, posture, and other communicative behaviors. You know this from your own experiences. Often, we may fail to communicate with words, but our actions or expressions still communicate to others. The nonverbal aspect of delivering a speech is just as important as the verbal delivery. This idea will be discussed in detail in a later chapter.

How does communication work? What makes a communication event, such as a speech, successful? The answer is in the process. Every time we speak to someone, every time we listen to someone, and every time we watch television or listen to the radio, we are involved in the communication process.

Let's examine this process. Since we are interested in public speaking, let's use a speaker and an audience for our example. First, communication always begins with someone who wants to send a message to a person or a group (Figure 1). If you are speaking with a

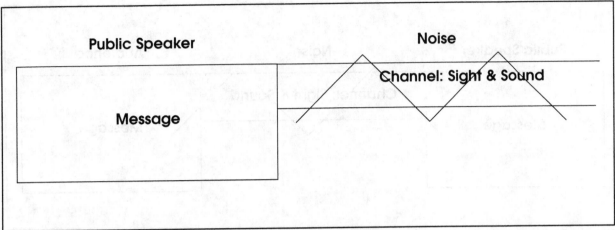

Figure 2. *Information is primarily received through sight and sound.*

friend, the information you provide represents the message. If you write a letter to someone, you are also sending a message. A public speaker is simply someone who provides information to other people.

Public Speaker

Once a public speaker determines the message or information he or she would like to share, the public speaker sends that information to the audience through a channel. Basically, a channel is a way to deliver a message to another person. So how does a public speaker send a message? He or she sends a message through one or more of our five senses. Our five senses are the only way we are able to receive information. If we cannot see it, hear it, taste it, touch it, or smell it, we cannot receive the information. Our primary means of receiving information is through sight and sound (Figure 2). Consider people who are both blind and deaf. Why is it so hard to communicate with them and teach them? The simple reason is two of the main communication channels are closed.

So, a channel is simply one or more of the five senses, and in a public speaking setting, we work mainly with sight and sound. We often think of a speech as only verbal communication (sound), yet sight is a great part of that communication. The audience can see you, and your appearance, facial expressions, and gestures help to convey your message and make it believable.

Unfortunately, our channels are often interrupted by noise. There are two kinds of noise: external and internal.

First, we all understand external noise, which can be any sounds that hinder us from understanding a message. In a public speaking setting, external noise is usually not a problem since the audience is quiet. We may have to contend with some kind of building problem, such as a loud air conditioner, but generally, we can control external noise.

The second kind of noise is more difficult to control. This noise is internal noise or mental noise. Internal noise happens inside of our bodies, and it can be a great hindrance to communication. Some examples are boredom, problems that claim our mental attention, or physical problems. For example, an audience member who has a

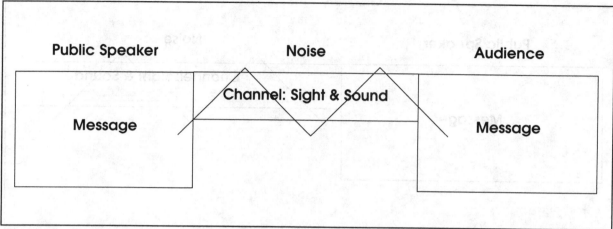

Figure 3. *Communication takes place if the message is understood after it is filtered through the noise.*

bad headache will probably not receive most of your communication. Internal noise is very difficult to control, so as a public speaker, one of your jobs is to provide a meaningful, interesting speech. A speech that is relevant, important, and sparks the interest of the audience will be able to overcome most internal noise (tactics for this will be discussed in the next three chapters).

After the speaker sends a message through a channel, it is filtered through various types of noise. Communication takes place if the audience understands the message after it has filtered through the noise (Figure 3).

There is one final aspect of this process: feedback. Feedback is information sent to the speaker that tells the speaker if the audience understands the message (Figure 4). In a public speaking setting, the feedback is usually nonverbal. Audience members may smile, nod their heads in agreement, or may avoid eye contact or expressions if they are bored or do not understand. If this happens, the speaker may need to restate a section that he or she has covered or possibly change to a different approach.

This book will show you how to write

and present an effective speech that will not receive negative feedback. If the audience is understanding and enjoying the speech, feedback can be a great confidence builder for the speaker. If not, it can be a tool that the speaker can use to improve his or her performance.

Both the channel and the feedback are interrupted by noise, since feedback travels along the same channel.

In summary, the purpose of communication is to always send an understandable message to another person or persons through one or more of the five senses. Noise interferes with that message, therefore, the two kinds of noise — external and internal — must be controlled. The receiver accepts the message and gives feedback to the sender, telling the sender if the message is understood. Keep these ideas in mind as you begin to develop your speech in Chapter Two.

There is one other communication concept you should understand. Realize that people can communicate unintentionally. A

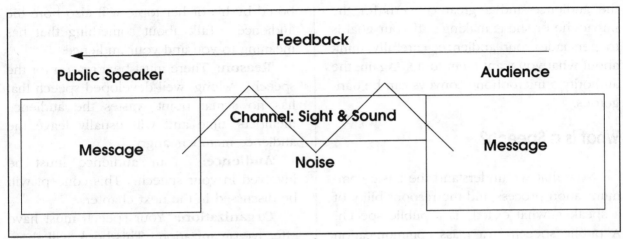

Figure 4. Feedback is information sent to the speaker.

gesture, a facial expression, or a nervous habit can communicate information to other people about your personality. In a public speaking situation, this may be a problem, and we will address this issue more closely in a later chapter.

Who Is a Speaker?

Now that we understand the basic communication process, let's discuss the communicator — you! There are some basic speaker responsibilities that you should understand before you begin the process of writing the speech.

Of course, we all know that freedom of speech is protected by the U.S. Constitution, but that freedom does not give a speaker the right to say anything he or she wishes. A sensitive, effective speaker keeps the following ideas in mind at all times from the writing of the speech to the delivery.

First, you, as the speaker, have the responsibility of honesty. The material in your speech, whether it is a major point or the smallest example, must be the truth. If you are using evidence, such as facts and statistics, that evidence must be gathered from credible sources. Chapter Three discusses the use of ethical evidence, so we will look at that more closely later.

Second, you are responsible for your treatment of other people. A microphone can be a dangerous weapon — one that can seriously hurt other people or their causes. A speaker should never use his or her power to degrade another person or group.

Third, a speaker has the responsibility to avoid racial or sexist language. A simple joke about a "dumb blonde" may get a few laughs from audience members, but your remark degrades people, and it will degrade you as a human being. Carefully watch for remarks in the text of your speech that may be considered racial or sexist.

Finally, the speaker has the responsibility of modesty. A speech is not a forum to build your personal ego, or spend time discussing your achievements. Remember that the purpose of a speech is to communicate a message — that message should not be you, the speaker. Realize that when you speak to an audience, you are morally and legally responsible for what you say. An ethical speaker will always have respect for the audience and a great concern for the impact he or she is making. If your goal is to persuade your audience, carefully think about what you want them to do. Again, the authority a microphone conveys can be dangerous.

What Is a Speech?

Now that we understand the basic communication process and the responsibility of a speaker, what exactly is a public speech? A public speech is a mass communication event, meaning that its purpose is to communicate with a large group of people. Simply put, the purpose of a speech is to provide important information that either teaches the members of the audience, persuades them to some action, or entertains them. A speech must be understandable to an audience, and it must connect with the audience members in some way that gives meaning to their lives. But, what is the difference between a good speech and a bad one? These are the deciding factors:

Belief: A good speech comes from a person who believes in what he or she is saying to the audience. A speaker who is bored by his or her topic will also bore the audience. Talk about something that has meaning to you and your audience.

Reason: There must be a reason for the speech. A long, well-developed speech that has no actual point wastes the audience members' time and will usually leave the audience members angry.

Audience: Your audience must be involved in your speech. This concept will be discussed in the next chapter.

Organization: Your speech must have effective organization. This book will show you how. . .

Color: Your speech should be full of interesting examples, language, humor, and hard-hitting ideas. We will learn how in the following chapters.

Delivery: You must be able to deliver your message to the audience —and yes, you will learn how.

Now we're ready to begin preparing for your speaking event. You are only a few chapters from an effective presentation. Remember, a good speech has the power to inspire people, the power to change them. It has the power to make a difference. So let's make that difference.

CHAPTER TWO

Who Is Your Audience?

There is an old story of a public speaker who was an excellent writer and presenter. His words and delivery style were dynamic; his voice was flawless. Once he delivered a speech to a large group of people. After the speech, one of the audience members came to him and said, "I thought you gave a good speech. I just wish it had something to do with me!"

Before you write the first word of your speech, you should consider your audience. Many speakers make the mistake of developing speeches that are ineffective simply because the content of the speech does not involve and include the audience. This does not mean that your speech topic has to be limited. You can give a successful speech on almost any subject to any group of people — if you connect with them. This chapter will show you how to make your speech relevant to your audience.

Audience Analysis

Whenever you attend a speaking occasion, you bring your life history with you. This includes your occupation, experiences, values, morals, and beliefs. Likewise, each audience member does the same. So, if everyone is unique, how can a speaker connect with everyone in the audience? The key is to discover the similarities. Study the model list shown in Figure 5.

Of course, this is not an exhaustive list of all the possible differences a group of people may have, but these ideas are the major ones that may impact the development of your speech.

When a journalist begins to work on a story, often he or she writes with a certain magazine in mind. That magazine has certain types of subscribers. For example, most subscribers to a cooking magazine will not also subscribe to a fishing magazine. The target audience of each magazine is different. So, the journalist does what is called **slanting.** Let's say the journalist wants to write an article about spending more time with children. The journalist will establish some principles about **quality time,** and begin to develop the article. Either the editor of the cooking magazine or the fishing magazine may be interested in the article, depending on the slant. The journalist may use examples of cooking with children to sell the article to the cooking magazine. If the journalist wants to sell to

SPEAKER	COMMUNICATION	AUDIENCE
Gender		Gender
Race		Race
Age		Age
Occupation		Occupation
Education		Education
Religion		Religion
Family life		Family life
Hobbies		Hobbies
Morals		Morals
Values		Values
Upbringing		Upbringing
Political beliefs		Political beliefs
Attitudes		Attitudes

Figure 5. *Sample audience analysis list.*

the fishing magazine, the journalist will use examples of fishing with children and the types of fishing children most enjoy. This idea also applies to speaking. If you want your audience to enjoy your speech, you must slant the speech to them.

After performing on the college speech circuit for several years, I was asked to give a speech to a civic organization in my hometown. Unfortunately, it asked for no specific topic. Additionally, all of the members were men, most were over forty years old, and all of them were involved in some type of business. I was twenty-three with a degree in speech and English. Obviously, the speech was difficult to write, but I was successful by using "audience analysis." I spoke about "uniqueness in America." I discussed some of my public speaking experiences, related them to different kinds of businesses in America, and made the main point that we are all individuals who all bring unique ideas to our community, city, and world. The speech was successful, and the audience members enjoyed themselves.

Before you begin to analyze your audience, you must first analyze yourself. To make this easier, let's create a speaker and an audience (Figure 6). Our speaker's name is Bob, and we will refer to him in the next several chapters as we develop some ideas that need an example. Study Bob's analysis, and

SPEAKER — BOB

Characteristic	*Response*
Gender:	Male
Race:	White
Age:	34
Occupation:	Banker
Education:	Bachelor's degree
Religion:	Protestant
Family Life:	Three children, all under ten years.
Hobbies:	Sports, camping, reading
Morals:	Strongly against drugs
Values:	Education, independence
Upbringing:	Rural
Political beliefs:	Conservative
Attitudes:	Believes in getting involved in community

Figure 6. Sample speaker analysis.

in your spiral notebook, write the characteristics and your response to each.

Now that you have your own analysis, let's begin to look at your audience. There will be some characteristics that you will be able to identify easily. You may discover others by speaking to someone within the group, or discussing the audience with someone in charge of the speaking event. If someone has asked you to speak and is in charge of the event, you should work with that person as you search for the answers. You may not find answers to every characteristic, and that is fine. Develop a list for your audience. For example, let's say that Bob, our speaker, will be speaking at a parent-teacher organization of some kind. Some of the audience's characteristics he might discover are shown in Figure 7.

As we can see from Bob's analysis, not all characteristics are known. In a group such as a parent-teacher organization, the occupations and education of the group will vary greatly. If you are preparing for a presentation within your company or business, this information will be much easier to obtain since most of the group will have a similar occupation and educational level.

AUDIENCE

Characteristic	Response
Gender:	85% female
Race:	Approximately 60% white, 40% black
Age:	Varies greatly. Most are between twenty-five and forty years old
Occupation:	Varies greatly, about 50% are professionals
Education:	Varies greatly, high school-graduate school
Religion:	Varies: most are of Protestant faiths
Family life:	All have children in the school system
Hobbies:	Unknown — no solid pattern
Morals:	Anti-drugs
Values:	Believe in active parenting and education
Upbringing:	Urban — 70% were born in the city
Political belief:	Unknown; however, a good guess would be conservative
Attitudes:	Like to be involved in activities, clubs, etc.

Figure 7. *Sample audience analysis.*

Slanting the Speech to the Audience

Now that you have your self analysis and your audience analysis, let's begin to look for areas that are similar. First, let's look for the strongest similar areas between you and your audience. In Bob's case, there are four definite areas: family life (children), morals (anti-drugs), values (belief in education), and attitudes (activism) (Figure 8).

As you study your list, you will see common areas emerge. You may not have this many. In fact, you may discover only one strong area. As Bob examines his list, he begins to see how he can slant his speech to this audience. Now, begin to rank these areas in order of importance. Bob's list would look like this:

1. *Children:* This is his strongest area. By using children and parenting examples, facts, or other information, he will connect with every person in the audience.

SPEAKER — BOB		AUDIENCE	
Characteristic	*Response*	*Characteristic*	*Response*
Gender:	Male	Gender:	85% female
Race:	White	Race:	Approximately 60% white, 40% black
Age:	34	Age:	Varies: Most between 25 – 40
Occupation:	Banker	Occupation:	About half are professionals
Education:	Bachelor's degree	Education:	Varies greatly
Religion:	Protestant	Religion:	Varies – most are of Protestant faiths
Family life:	Three children, all under ten	Family life:	All have children in school
Hobbies:	Sports, camping, reading	Hobbies:	Unknown — no solid pattern
Morals:	Anti-drugs	Morals:	Anti-drugs
Values:	Education independence	Values:	Active parenting, education
Upbringing:	Rural	Upbringing:	Urban — 70% were born in the city
Political belief:	Conservative	Political belief:	Unknown
Attitudes:	Involved in community	Attitudes:	Like to be involved in activities

Figure 8. *Comparing speaker analysis to audience analysis.*

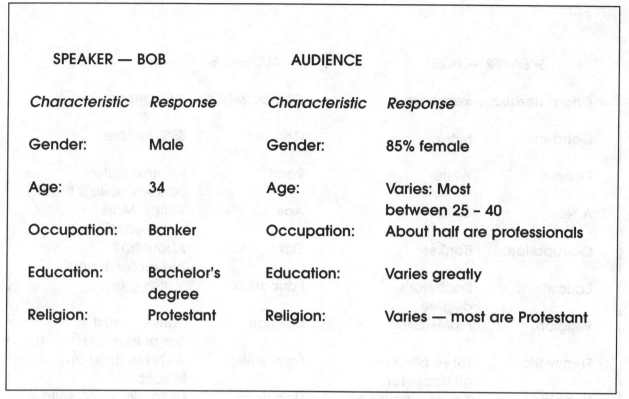

Figure 9. *Secondary areas.*

2. *Anti-drugs:* Any anti-drug examples or facts will further connect him with his audience and cause the audience to believe his ideas.

3. *School:* Examples of effective education or successful children will be appreciated and appropriate in his speech.

4. *Activism:* Examples of people getting involved in their community, city, or country will work well. After all, that is why his audience is attending this meeting.

These are Bob's strongest slant areas. He should keep them in mind constantly as he develops his speech. Again, this does not mean that Bob's idea for a topic or the topic given to him must be changed in any way. This information simply means that Bob's examples and support material need to relate to these areas.

Now that you have the strongest areas for your slant, let's look at some of the others. These areas are called secondary areas, but they are still important to consider. Continue creating the list you have started.

Let's look at Bob's secondary areas. His including gender, age, occupation, education, and religion (Figure 9).

5. *Gender:* Although Bob is a male, and most of his audience is female, this area is still important. Remember, the audience members have children, so any stories or examples about the importance of motherhood will be appropriate and connect with his audience.

6. *Age:* This may not directly affect Bob's speech, but at least he knows that most of the audience members are close to his age.

SPEAKER — BOB		AUDIENCE	
Characteristic	*Response*	*Characteristic*	*Response*
Race:	White	Race:	Approximately 60% white, 40% black
Hobbies:	Sports, camping, reading	Hobbies:	Unknown — no solid pattern
Upbringing:	Rural	Upbringing:	Urban — 70% were born in the city
Political Belief:	Conservative	Political Belief:	Unknown

Figure 10. *Negative areas.*

7.   *Occupation:* If Bob needs to talk about occupations, he should use several examples, from blue-collar to white-collar occupations, since his audience members have various types of jobs.

8.   *Education:* Again, this area varies greatly, so Bob should use various examples if he needs to include education in his speech.

9. *Religion:* This is similar to number 8. Bob may not need this information, but at least he knows that most of his audience is religious if he needs this information as he develops his speech.

So far, Bob has nine important areas that affect his speech, with a special emphasis on the first four.

How is your list? Hopefully, you have discovered some very important similarities that will affect your speech.

Finally, let's look at the last several areas. These are negative areas that Bob would not want to use in his speech. We use "negative" to mean these areas will not directly enhance the speech. You probably have several negative areas left over. Let's look at Bob's negative ares (Figure 10) so we can understand why he would not want to use these areas.

First, Bob's race is not a factor in this audience analysis. Although over half of the audience is white, the audience is still mixed, so there are a number of cultural differences. Even if the audience had been all white, Bob would never want to make any kind of racist comments, jokes, or statements. Remember the discussion we had earlier about speaker ethics. The point is simply that the race of the audience is not important for his speech development. If all of the audience members had been of a different race than Bob, he might want to use some specific examples from that culture. Since that is not the case in this instance, the issue of race is not a factor.

Next, Bob and the audience do not share specific hobbies or leisure activities. There may be some audience members who enjoy camping or sports, but since Bob does not know this information, he would not want to use a large number of sports or wilderness examples in his speech. Since this is an interest to Bob, he may use some examples, but he should be aware that this is not a strong area.

Third, Bob grew up in the country, and most of his audience grew up in the city. He would not want to use many examples of life on the farm, since his audience will not relate to his experience.

Finally, the political beliefs of the audi-ence vary, so this is not a strong area for the speech. Bob may know a great Democrat joke, but he runs the risk of offending many of the members of his audience, so he would want to remain politically neutral.

At this point, you should have a working list of strengths and weaknesses for your speech development. Again, the purpose of an audience analysis is not to change the speech topic or make you appear to be someone you are not. The purpose is to give you a list of areas that will help you, the speaker, relate to the audience.

Now that you understand your audience, we are ready to begin working on the speech. Keep your audience analysis in mind as we begin. We will refer to it again and again as we work on your speech. Remember, making a connection with each audience member is the best way to make the speech important to each person, the way to inhibit internal noise, and the way to leave your audience feeling satisfied and glad that they had an opportunity to hear you.

CHAPTER THREE

Getting Started

A blank sheet of paper can send chills through even the most experienced speaker's spine. The task of writing a speech is difficult at best, and getting started is the most difficult part of the writing process. This chapter will ease your chill and provide a step-by-step approach to writing an effective speech. I strongly recommend that you work on your speech as you read the next four chapters. Simply reading over these chapters will not help you. In fact, it may actually confuse you, so get your pen and paper ready.

As I stated in Chapter One, this book is designed to take you step-by-step through the preparation of the speech. As you begin to write your speech, you should remember that there are many types of speeches. Some speeches seek to persuade an audience, others teach the audience something, and others fulfill some special role, such as presenting an award to another person.

Because of these differences, speeches basically fall into two major categories: **regular speeches** and **special speeches.**

A regular speech is fundamentally what we think of when we say the word **speech.** A regular speech includes informative, persuasive, and entertainment speaking, and more than likely, you are preparing a regular speech for an event. Some common examples of regular speeches are keynote addresses, political speeches, luncheon or banquet speeches, and general speeches given in a place of business about sales, expenses, new products, and so forth.

Special speeches are simply speeches that are specialized to do a certain job — such as demonstrating a new product, presenting an award, accepting an award or position, and others in this category. If you are preparing a special speech, Chapter Five will show you the actual writing process; however, this chapter and Chapter Four will provide you with valuable information. If you are preparing a regular speech, then continue to read and follow the instructions in the next two chapters.

The Basic Speech Model

Let's take a few moments to understand the structure of a regular speech. Unlike something you read, a speech is **delivered,** and the way it is written is different from other types of writing. Remember that a speech is sent through two channels as discussed in Chapter One. First, there is a visual channel, and secondly, there is an auditory channel. The actual writing of the speech is concerned with the auditory delivery, and since a speech is auditory, there are certain parts of a speech that must be present and clear in order for an audience to fully understand it. Consider the following model, then let's discuss each part before we actually begin writing.

THE BASIC SPEECH MODEL

    I. Introduction
          TRANSITION

    II. Speech Body
      A. The first point
          TRANSITION
      B. The second point
          TRANSITION
      C. The third point
          TRANSITION

    III. Conclusion

As you can see, there are three basic parts of a speech: the **introduction,** the **body,** and the **conclusion.** The body contains three to five points or main ideas, and between each of these sections, there is a **transition,** or a statement that leads the audience to the next section.

Most people have problems writing a speech because they begin writing in the wrong place — the beginning. The introduction, especially the opening sentences, is the most difficult to write, and many speakers develop severe writer's block before they write the first word. We will take a different approach to writing the speech — we will write it out of order, and this is the approach that most good speakers take. So, let's begin.

The Topic

Before you begin writing, you must have a solid topic and purpose. You may have a topic that has been given to you, or the topic may be entirely your choice. If you are giving a presentation, you most likely have been provided with a topic. Generally, presentations are given to a specific group about a specific issue. A speech, however, may vary. If the speech topic is your choice, then you need to spend some time thinking about it now. If you are undecided, look back at your audience analysis notes. What are some possible topics that your audience would enjoy? Make a list of possible topics and think about each one.

Let's consider Bob's speech. Let's say that Bob has an **open** topic, meaning he may speak about any issue. Since Bob is speaking at a parent-teacher meeting, some basic ideas emerge: education, children, success in school, and parental involvement. Any of these topics might work, but Bob can further narrow his list by looking at his audience analysis. Remember that Bob's strongest areas of interest between him and his audience are children, concerns about drug abuse in the school and community, education, and involvement in the community.

So, Bob might create some speech topics from this list such as "raising drug-free children," "raising successful children," "making a difference in our school," or "raising children who are active learners." Bob can look at this second list and consider his choices. First, "raising drug-free children" would be a good topic, but Bob is not an expert in drug abuse or the methods for protecting children, so this topic would not be his best choice. The topic "raising successful children" is interesting, but a little too broad. "Making a difference in our school" and "raising children who are active learners" are both good choices, but Bob chooses the second for his speech topic because he can talk about the importance of getting involved in school and how that leads to success. So, he has linked three of his strongest areas: children, education, and involvement.

As you are deciding your topic, consider four important points:

1. *Talk about something you find interesting and have some expertise.* Even though you may have a good topic that you believe your audience will enjoy, you must be personally interested in the issue or you will not do a good job. Yes, consider your audience analysis, but in the end, you must pick a topic that interests you and in which you have knowledge.

2. *Make sure your topic is not too general.* For example, "freedom in America"

sounds good, but you could talk for years about this topic alone. Try to narrow your topic down to some specifics. A broad topic will confuse you and your audience.

3. *Do not be too specific.* Although you want to avoid an overly general topic, you also want to avoid a topic that is so narrow you cannot develop it. For example, "the many colors of roses" may sound good, but can you really develop a speech concerned only with the color of various rose bushes? Probably not.

4. *Finally, keep your topic to one main idea.* You would be unable to effectively develop a speech that has a number of major ideas. For example, "the breeds, care, feeding, and training of dogs" has too many ideas to cover during one speech. Keep it to one major idea.

Once you have developed your topic, write one sentence in your spiral notebook stating your topic. Bob would write:

**TOPIC: Raising children who
are active learners.**

If you cannot write one sentence, then you need to spend time thinking about your topic. I'm reminded of a company worker who approached the company president with a plan to increase production. The president handed him a business card and said, "Write your plan on the back of this." The worker replied that the little business card did not have enough space to write his plan. The president said, "Then you do not have a plan yet. Keep thinking." The same is true with your speech topic. **Do not** continue to the next section until you can write one simple sentence stating your speech topic.

The Purpose

Now that you have a solid topic for your speech, let's develop your purpose. A topic alone can take on many forms, so you must decide how you will approach this topic.

Again, let's refer to Bob as our example. Bob's topic, raising children who are active learners, can be approached from many angles. As Bob thinks about his approach, he begins to list several possibilities. You should develop a list as well. Let's say that Bob, after thinking about his topic, discovers the following approaches:

```
1. My speech will inform
   the audience about meth-
   ods for developing
   active learners.
2. My speech will inform
   the audience about the
   need for developing
   active learners.
3. My speech will persuade
   the audience that all
   children need to be
   active learners.
4. My speech will inform
   the audience about the
   benefits of active learning.
```

Of course, this is not an exhaustive list of the possible approaches to active learning, and your list will not be exhaustive either, but you will at least have a number of approaches. Notice that the possible approaches above are phrased in **one sentence**. Again, you must have one specific purpose in mind and stick to that one purpose so that your speech accomplishes a goal.

As you think about the purpose for your speech, consider these important points:

1. Do you want to *inform* your audience (teach them something) or *persuade* your audience (get them to do something)?

2. Out of all of the possible approaches, in which do you have the most knowledge and interest? For example, a "how-to" speech about gardening may be easier to develop than a speech discussing the benefits of gardening.

3. What do you really want your audience to leave "knowing?"

Think about these areas and decide on an approach. Once you have the approach, write it in your notebook. Bob's example so far would look like this:

```
TOPIC: Raising children who
       are active learners.
PURPOSE: To inform the
       audience about the
       methods for develop
       ing active learners.
```

As in the first section, **do not** continue until you have a purpose phrased in a single sentence.

The Body

Now that we have a topic and a purpose, let's begin working on your speech. We will begin your speech by first developing the **middle,** or the body of the speech. The body is the main crux of your speech. Essentially, it covers everything you want to say during your speech. In other words, the body is the content. How you write this section will determine if your speech will be successful. But don't worry, this book will guide you through your writing.

As discussed earlier, a body has three to five main points or ideas. Remember that a speech is delivered, so our organizational methods are different from other types of writing. The content of your speech must be remembered by your audience, since there will be nothing they can refer to once it is over. For example, as you read this book, you can always refer to another chapter or section. But with a speech, you have one chance and one chance only to get your message across to the audience.

For this reason, a speech is most effective when it uses **point development.** Once your speech is complete, your audience will primarily remember your main points, so what you choose for your main points is most important. First, I recommend that you use only three points. Your audience will more easily remember three major ideas than five. You want the audience to remember your speech, so this is the best approach. You may have more points, and that is fine, but make sure your points do not overlap. For example, if you were giving a speech about the care of dogs, you may have four main points such as (1) feeding, (2) health, (3) grooming, and (4) training. Although these are different areas, health and grooming can be combined. Grooming is a part of a dog's health because it controls pests and protects the hair and skin, so the speech could still function with feeding, health, and training. You have not cut any information; you have just organized it differently.

So, begin to think about the major points you will discuss. Let's look again at Bob's speech. After carefully considering his topic and purpose, Bob decides on three major points and writes them down:

TOPIC: Raising children
who are active
learners.
PURPOSE: To inform the
audience about
the methods for
developing active
learners.

MAIN POINTS:
1. Teach them to ask
questions.
2. Teach them responsi
bility.
3. Teach them organiza
tional skills.

Once Bob has his list, he carefully thinks about the points. You should do the same. As you look at your points, ask yourself these questions:

1. Are the points too general or too specific?
2. Are the points closely related?
3. Do the points support the topic and purpose?
4. Are the points what I really want the audience to know?

After considering these questions, Bob decides his points need some revision. You may have discovered this as well. Let's take a look at Bob's revised list and see the changes he has made. First, Bob's points are closely related, so he is okay on this part. However, he discovers that one point is more specific than the others. Iin fact, it is too specific, and he may have a difficult time writing the section. So, Bob revises his list, and now he has:

1. **Teach them to participate.**
2. **Teach them responsibility.**
3. **Teach them organizational skills.**

The revised first point is better because it is more general. This gives Bob a number of ideas to discuss, one of them being "learn to ask questions." Bob again examines his list and discovers that these three points are strong and important for his audience. At this time, you should have your main points for the speech body. Again, each point should be only a word or phrase which focuses on one item. Do not continue to the next section until you have your main points ready.

Organizing Your Points

Now that your main points are ready, we need to look at them again for possible organizational revisions. Let's plug Bob's points into our model:

I. Introduction
    TRANSITION

II. Speech Body
    A. Teach them participation skills.
       TRANSITION
    B. Teach them responsibility skills.
       TRANSITION
    C. Teach them organizational skills.
       TRANSITION

III. Conclusion

According to the model, Bob will talk about these three main points in the order shown above. But that order may not be best. There is no definite formula for point organization, but the speech topic, or simply the speaker's preference, may dictate a certain point order. Some speakers like to talk about the most important point first, while others prefer to talk about the most important point last. Or, your topic may require a certain order. For example, let's say that a sales representative is talking about a new computer program with these three main points:

1. Program capabilities.
2. Integration with current programs.
3. Using the program in your business.

For this speech, the three points must remain in the current order. Audience members cannot understand how the program can be integrated with other programs if they do not understand what the program does. Also, audience members cannot understand how to use the program in their businesses if they do not understand how it can be integrated with existing applications.

As Bob thinks about his speech, he decides to reorganize his points. Bob feels that a student must be organized before he or she can learn responsibility skills or how to fully participate in school, so Bob decides to talk about organizational skills first. Next, Bob decides to talk about participation skills because he can refer to organization and participation skills as he talks about his third point, responsibility. With this new organization, his topics easily lead to one another. So, Bob rearranges his speech:

I. Introduction
    TRANSITION

II. Speech Body
    A. Teach them organizational skills
       TRANSITION
    B. Teach them participation skills
       TRANSITION
    C. Teach them responsibility skills
       TRANSITION

III. Conclusion

Rearrange any points you feel need moving at this time. If you are unsure about your point order, just leave the points as they are for the time being. You may discover a better organization after you begin writing, and you can always reorganize your points at that time. Once you are satisfied with your points and their order, you are ready to begin writing your text. You may feel tired at this point, and that's okay. You have just completed the most difficult part of speech writing.

Developing Your Points

Before we begin developing your points and writing your text, let's discuss an important item. First, I want to dispel a myth. You may have heard a saying like, "Never write out a speech. Give it from your heart, not from your paper." This is a noble idea, but speeches that are not written out never sound like they come from the heart; instead, they sound like they come from mass confusion. You may have

some questions about using a **script** or a written speech, or just a few notes when you perform. This topic will be discussed in detail later on. For now, you need to write out your speech, just as you would write out a paper for an English class.

There is a common misconception that a speaker should decide his or her major ideas for discussion, and the rest will "fall into place." **This will not happen.** Speeches that are given "off the top of the head" sound like they are given "off the top of the head." You will sound unprepared and incompetent, and this is not what you want your audience to remember about you or the speech. So keep writing!

Essentially, the purpose of the speech body is to discuss the main points. Simply put, **give the information, provide evidence, and give examples.** Let's discuss the second two: evidence and examples.

Generally, a speaker needs additional evidence and examples to back up the main points given during a speech. Even if a famous doctor is discussing his latest findings in heart surgery, he would still quote other famous doctors or researchers to back up his statements. This is known as evidence. Depending on the type of speech you are giving, you may need more or less evidence. If you are discussing the structure of an atom, you will need to quote what a number of experts have said about the atom. If you are giving a speech about the importance of sports for children, you would need less evidence to support your opinions.

Let's discuss the types of evidence. Generally, evidence consists of facts, statistics, and statements or quotes given by experts on the subject. First, a fact is some piece of information that can be proven. For example, it is a fact that gravity exists. Secondly, statistics are studies which give percentage information. For example, "Research shows that 79% of the population would like to earn more money." Statistics are good and may back up your point, but be careful not to overuse them. Statistics can often be refuted by other researchers, so they are not always "strong" evidence. Also, you do not want your speech so full of statistical quotes that it sounds like a stock market analysis. Finally, statements or quotes by experts or professionals in the field are always good and appropriate. Again, do not overuse quotes; it is still your speech.

So how do you use evidence? Again, let's look at Bob's speech body:

II. Speech Body
    A. Teach them organizational skills.
    1. How will this help? Explain the purpose of organizational skills for active learning.
    2. Will this really work? Provide evidence/proof and give examples.
    3. How? Explain how to teach the skills.

TRANSITION

    B. Teach them to participate in school.
    1. How will this help? Explain the purpose of participation skills for active learning.
    2. Will this really work? Provide evidence/proof and give examples.
    3. How? Explain how to teach the skills.

TRANSITION

    C. Teach them responsibility.
    1. How will this help? Explain the purpose of responsibilty skills for active learning.
    2. Will this really work? Provide evidence/proof and give examples.
    3. How? Explain how to teach the skills.

With Bob's topic, he must explain the purpose of the skills, provide evidence and examples, then explain how to teach a child the skills. Remember that evidence can be any combination of things as long as the evidence comes from credible sources and supports the main points. Bob would want to use a number of quotes, some from expert teachers, some from parents who have successful learners, and possibly some facts about the effect of active learning on success in later life. As Bob writes, he should constantly remember that his goal is to prove to the audience that each skill is vitally important, and he must explain to audience members how to teach the skills to their children.

As you begin to write each section of the body, keep these items in mind:

1. *Research material such as facts and statistics can be gathered from your local library.* With the use of CD-ROM and other computerized services, research has become very quick and easy. Just make sure that your research information comes from credible sources such as experts and national news magazines. You should avoid tabloids or any sources that present questionable information. Ask a librarian to help you if you are not sure how to search for the information.

2. *As you write your points, they may sound boring.* That is fine for now. Remember that this is a first draft. A later chapter in this book

will help you make the speech more interesting and give it more flavor.

3. *If you begin to get stuck, go back to the purpose statement that you developed earlier.* What exactly do you want your audience to know?

4. *Do not worry about transitions or making each point connect together.* We will work on that later.

5. *Be aware of your time limits.* Do you have 10 minutes or 30 minutes? Keep this in mind as you write your speech.

6. *Keep your audience analysis in mind.* As you look for quotes and other evidence, remember your strong areas and use these to connect with the audience. This will be dis-cussed further in Chapter Six.

As you work on the speech body, stop occasionally and read your material out loud. Listen to yourself and the flow of your sentences. This will give you some direction as you work.

Remember, the speech body is the main part of your speech. Finish the first draft of the speech body before you go to the next chapter. Once you finish the first draft, you may want to **time** it to see how you are doing on your time limit so far. Also, there are two sample speeches in Appendix A at the end of this book. You may want to refer to these examples as you work on the speech body.

CHAPTER FOUR

Completing Your First Draft

There's an old adage that says, "No matter what you do, always start and end with grace." This is good advice for a public speaker. This chapter will help you develop your **introduction,** your **conclusion,** and your **transitions.** By the time you finish this chapter, you will have your first draft of the complete speech. Remember that the speech body is the main part of your speech. In essence, everything that you want your audience to know is given in the speech body. This does not mean that the introduction and conclusion are not important. In fact, an audience will not listen to the speech body if you do not have an effective introduction. So let's begin work.

The Introduction

The **introduction** contains three major parts: introductory statements, the main topic or thesis, and the major points that you will discuss in your speech body. As noted in the last chapter, the introductory statements are often the most difficult to write. Basically, you want to begin your speech with a hook or something that will capture the audience's attention. You have probably heard speakers who begin with a joke, then say, "but seriously folks...." This is not what you should do. Although you can use almost any type of introductory statement, such as a joke, effectively, your introductory statement should lead naturally into your speech and not exist on its own. Let's take a look at some types of introductory statements.

Quotes: Quotes from famous people are always a good way to begin a speech, especially if the quote is humorous in nature. However, **do not** give a quote just for the sake of giving a quote. The statement must naturally lead into the content of your speech. For example, let's say that you are giving a speech on the qualities of success.

A good introductory statement might be, "Amelia Earhart once said, 'Courage is the price that life exacts for granting peace.'" This quote captures the audience's attention and leads directly into the content of the speech. Remember that quotes are often very general in nature. If you are giving a speech about thermonuclear energy, you might have a hard time finding a quote about the subject, but you would still be able to relate many quotes to that topic. For example, "The most simple things in life are often the most complex," would be a good opening quote for this speech. A number of books that contain quotes, stories, and jokes especially for speakers are available. See the Resources section at the end of this book for a list of helpful ideas.

Stories: Many speakers prefer to begin their speeches with a short story of some kind. Often, these stories can come from your own experiences or from something you have heard or read in the past. Stories are very effective as introductory statements if you keep two rules in mind. First, keep it short. A story to introduce your topic should be less than one minute long. Second, make sure it directly relates to your speech topic. Again, **never** introduce a speech with a story just for the sake of sharing a story.

Jokes: Jokes are one of the most popular means of introducing a speech. However, there are a few points to keep in mind before deciding to use a joke. First, is the joke funny? Will it be funny to the audience? This is a difficult question since different people have different senses of humor, so you must consider using a joke carefully. Nothing is worse than beginning a speech with a joke that no one finds humorous. Secondly, is the joke appropriate? Remember, some jokes are offensive, especially if they use sexist or racial language, and often a joke may be offensive to some people even if it is not to you. Again, be careful. Finally, as with the other types of introductory statements, does it directly relate to the speech topic?

You should choose one of these three methods for your opening statements. You should never begin a speech by saying, "Hello. My speech is about..." or "Today we will talk about...." You want to capture your audience's attention, not bore them from the start. Remember to consult the Resources section for sources that contain interesting introduction information.

Building an Introduction

Let's return, once again, to Bob's speech for our example. Since Bob's topic is "raising children who are active learners," he wants to capture the audience's attention right from the start. After considering quotes, stories, and jokes, Bob decides that he is more comfortable using a quote. He looks for quotes and soon finds one that easily relates to his topic. He writes the quote and makes a few comments about it so that it relates to his topic. Let's look at his introductory statements:

```
    Stephen Leacock once said,
"I am a great believer in luck
— and I find that the harder I
work, the more I have of it."
We all know there is a lot of
truth in that statement. As I
have worked in the banking
business for the past eight
```

years, I have discovered that the key to success is simply hard work.

Yet, as parents and teachers, we often think differently about school. Perhaps you have heard statements like, "Johnny is just smart, so he does well in school," or "Susie likes to participate in class, so the teachers always like her." But the simple fact of the matter is that learners are not born; they are developed. Students are not successful in school because of luck. They are successful because they have been taught skills which enable them to work hard and to be successful every day.

Bob opens the speech with the quote, discusses the idea, and relates the idea to his topic of raising active learners.

Now that Bob has his introductory statements, he is ready to move on to the next section of the introduction — his topic statement. Bob simply takes his topic statement and adds it to the introductory statements he has already written. Notice how the introductory statements lead directly to his topic. The audience knows at this point exactly what his speech will be about. All too often, speakers give long presentations that leave the audience wondering, "What was the point?" Look again at Bob's introduction, and let's add the topic statement.

Stephen Leacock once said, "I am a great believer in luck

— and I find that the harder I work, the more I have of it." We all know there is a lot of truth in that statement. As I have worked in the banking business for the past eight years, I have discovered that the key to success is simply hard work.

Yet, as parents and teachers, we often think differently about school. Perhaps you have heard statements like, "Johnny is just smart, so he does well in school," or "Susie likes to participate in class, so the teachers always like her." But the simple fact of the matter is that learners are not born; they are developed. Students are not successful in school because of luck. They are successful because they have been taught skills which enable them to work hard and to be successful every day.

So let's spend some time talking about how each of us, as parents, can teach our children to be active learners.

Notice how the topic statement is direct so that the audience knows exactly what Bob will discuss.

Now that you have your introductory statements and your topic statement, simply add your major points that you developed in Chapter Three. Speech teachers often say, "In a speech, you tell them what you are going to tell them, tell them about it, then tell them what you have told them." A little confusing maybe, but that statement is true. Before you begin your speech body, you should tell your audience the major ideas you are going to discuss. Remember that as you speak, you must help your audience stay with you and keep it from getting confused. One way you can do this is to help the audience members create a mental outline of your speech. So, you should begin forming this mental outline in your introduction.

As Bob completes his introduction, he adds his three main points. Notice how they are stated.

> Stephen Leacock once said, "I am a great believer in luck — and I find that the harder I work, the more I have of it." We all know there is a lot of truth in that statement. As I have worked in the banking business for the past eight years, I have discovered that the key to success is simply hard work.
>
> Yet, as parents and teachers, we often think differently about school. Perhaps you have heard statements like, "Johnny is just smart, so he does well in school," or "Susie likes to participate in class, so the teachers always like her." But the simple fact of the matter is that learners are not born; they are developed. Students are not successful in school because of luck. They are successful because they have been taught skills which enable them to work hard and to be successful every day.
>
> So let's spend some time talking about how each of us, as parents, can teach our children to be active learners. First, We will discuss how to teach children organizational skills. Second, we will talk about participation skills. Finally, we will take a look at responsibility.

Notice that Bob's three main points are directly stated and in the order he will discuss each.

This is an example of an effective introduction. It will capture the audience's attention and give a mental outline of what's to come in the speech. Notice that this introduction is not very long — an introduction shouldn't be. Remember that your purpose is to introduce the topic, and long, complex introductions usually lose the audience from the beginning. Complete your introduction at this time. Compare what you have written to the model above, and do not move on to the next section until your introduction is complete.

The Transitions

A transition is a sentence that moves the audience from one section of the speech to the next. This is sometimes called **sign posting** among public speakers. For example, if you are driving in an unfamiliar city, you often depend on street signs to direct your way. A speech is the same. Although the topic is not new to you by the time you present the speech, it is new to the audience. The speech is like driving in unfamiliar territory to them, and you need to help them stay on the right track. This is the second method for keeping the audience members' attention and helping them not to get confused as they listen to you. Additionally, transitions add to the mental outline we began to create in the introduction. Look, once again, at the basic speech model:

I. Introduction
    TRANSITION

II. Speech Body
    A. The first point
        TRANSITION
    B. The second point
        TRANSITION
    C. The third point
        TRANSITION

III. Conclusion

Notice that you need a transition in between each new section. There are no definite formulas for writing transition statements. Just remember that your purpose is to lead your audience from one section to the next, and a transition statement should be only one sentence. Let's examine Bob's speech. The transitions are in bold type and explanations for each are in brackets.

[Introduction] Stephen Leacock once said, "I am a great believer in luck — and I find that the harder I work, the more I have of it." We all know there is a lot of truth in that statement. As I have worked in the banking business for the past eight years, I have discovered that the key to success is simply hard work.

Yet, as parents and teachers, we often think differently about school. Perhaps you have heard statements like, "Johnny is just smart, so he does well in school," or "Susie likes to participate in class, so the teachers always like her." But the simple fact of the matter is that learners are not born; they are developed. Students are not successful in school because of luck. They are successful because they have been taught skills which enable them to work hard and to be successful every day.

So let's spend some time talking about how each of us, as parents, can teach our children to be active learners. First, we will discuss how to teach children organizational skills. Second, we will talk about participation skills. Finally, we will take a look at responsibility.

[The speech body. Point 1 — Transition]
If we truly want our children to be active learners in

school, we must first teach them a skill we all need — organization.

[This statement leads the audience from the introduction directly to his first point. Bob would discuss this point as explained in Chapter Three, and once he finishes, he would move to the next transition.]

[The speech body. Point 2 — Transition]

Although organization is very important for success in school, a child must be a part of the class, which brings us to our second point, participation skills.

[Notice how the transition connects the two areas and reminds the audience of the mental outline he established in the introduction. Bob would discuss this point, and move on to the next transition once he has finished discussing participation.]

[The speech body. Point 3 — Transition]

With organization and participation skills, a child can be successful, but we still need one final skill to make the child an active learner, and that skill is responsibility.

[The transition relates the first two points to the last point and leads the audience to his final topic. Once he has finished this discussion, he is ready to move to his conclusion.]

[Conclusion — Transition]

As parents and teachers, we all must strive to raise active learners.

[This statement leaves the discussion of how to teach children the three skills to a more general approach, thus opening the door for his conclusion.]

At this point, place your introduction and body points in order and develop your transitions to connect each section. Once you finish, move on to the next section. Then we will develop your conclusion.

The Conclusion

The word **conclusion** is always good to hear because it means you are almost finished! A speech conclusion consists of three major parts: restating your points, the final punch, and a concluding statement or statements. Generally, a conclusion is rather easy, since most of it has already been done in other parts of your speech.

First, restate your main points. This step completes your audience's mental outline and reemphasizes your points one last time. Let's begin to develop Bob's conclusion as an example. He writes his points in past tense, since he has already discussed these ideas.

Today we have discussed three skills children need to be active learners: organization, participation, and responsibility. We have also discussed a number of methods to develop these skills.

[Bob restates the three main points and

gives a one-sentence summary of the overall purpose of the speech.]

Next, we use what I call the **final punch.** Basically, this is a one-sentence statement that hits the audience with the most important idea of your speech. It is your last chance to influence your audience, and this statement is one of the main ones it will remember. Bob's would look like this:

> Today we have discussed
> three skills children need to
> be active learners: organiza-
> tion, participation, and
> responsibility. We have also
> discussed a number of methods
> to develop these skills. If we
> truly want our children to be
> successful in life, they must
> be active learners in the
> classroom.

[This is a final punch statement about the basic content of the speech.]

Finally, we come to the last line(s) of the speech, or the concluding statements. Ideally, this statement or statements should do what I call **tying.** Simply put, the concluding lines should tie the speech together by relating directly to the opening statements in the introduction. This is difficult to do at times, but this method creates a strong conclusion. Let's complete Bob's conclusion.

> Today we have discussed
> three skills children need to
> be active learners: organiza-
> tion, participation, and

responsibility. We have also
discussed a number of methods
to develop these skills. If we
truly want our children to be
successful in life, they must
be active learners in the
classroom. After all, a little luck in life is always
nice, but our work ethic is
the real test of our success.
[Ties directly to the opening quote.]

Sample Introduction and Conclusion

To help you further, examine the introduction and conclusion that follow. This text is from a speech I delivered during the late 1980s about African elephant extinction. This speech is rather complex, and the introduction is a little long, but you will see examples of evidence in the introduction and a solid establishment of the topic and purpose. Examine the parts of the introduction and conclusion and notice how the two tie together:

> Bill Woodley killed his
> first elephant when he was 16
> years old. By the time he was
> 19, he had killed 150 more and
> made his living as a profes-
> sional ivory hunter. But
> today, at age 60, Bill Woodley
> is an elephant protector. In
> the October 16, 1989 issue of
> *Time* magazine he said, "They
> say once an elephant hunter,
> always an elephant hunter,
> but I've spent the past 41
> years hunting poachers."
> The great animal with the

long, swinging trunk and huge, pendulous ears is certainly no stranger to the American public. As a child, I can remember frequent trips to the zoo to see the elephant, and Walt Disney's "Dumbo — The Flying Elephant" was always one of my favorites.

But in the near future, children and adults may not have the opportunity to enjoy these gentle beasts. According to the African Wildlife Foundation in Washington, D.C., by the year 2000, the African elephant may be totally extinct. The extinction will be caused by poaching — an insatiable greed for "white gold," or the tusks of elephants, otherwise known as ivory.

Over the years, many species of animals have become extinct due to natural causes, but the African elephant is one species that is in danger because of mankind. According to *Time* magazine, October 16, 1989, if we lose the elephant species, we will probably lose at least 30 other species in Africa, creating what Richard Leakey, director of Kenya's Department of Wildlife Services, calls one of the greatest ecosystem disasters that mankind has ever known.

In order to understand this problem and the immediate action that we must take, I would like for us to take a look at the illegal ivory industry, the current action being taken against poachers, and finally, how we, as individuals, can help save this species.

[At this point, the speech body is delivered consisting of the three main points: the ivory industry, the current action being taken, and how individuals can help save the species. Now read the conclusion.]

In understanding this problem and the action we must take, we have looked at the illegal ivory industry, the current action being taken against poachers, and finally, how we can help save this species by refusing to buy ivory, refusing to buy products from stores who sell ivory, and by telling other people about this problem.

Our involvement in this problem may determine whether or not the elephant species will still exist in the year 2000. For unless we reduce the demand for ivory in this country, the only way future generations may know of these great animals may simply be Dumbo — just a fictitious animal in a storybook.

Notice the connection between the introduction and conclusion with the "Dumbo" statements. Although the introduction uses two forms of introductory statements (a story and a personal experience), the conclusion directly relates to the introduction and is a solid, hard-hitting statement.

As you finish your first draft, let me congratulate you! You have just completed one of the most difficult parts of public speaking. As you read over your first draft, you may notice many errors, awkward sounding sections, or parts that just seem dry. Don't worry — we will turn your first draft into a first-rate speech. Before you move on to the next chapter, let's check your speech once again. Look at your speech and answer the following questions. If you cannot answer "yes" to every question, you may need to make a few changes.

1. Did you begin with an attention getter?

2. Is there a sentence in your introduction which tells the audience exactly what your speech will be about?

3. Did you state the main points in your introduction?

4. Do your transition statements tie the speech together so that your speech naturally flows from one idea to the next?

5. Did you restate the main points in your conclusion?

6. Do your concluding lines directly relate to your introduction in some way?

If you can answer "yes" to all of these questions, then let's begin polishing your speech and creating your final draft.

CHAPTER FIVE

Special Speeches

Chapters Three and Four examined the basic speech model that can be adapted to virtually any type of speech for any occasion. There are, however, some **special speeches** that do not fit the basic model. This chapter examines and provides examples of four kinds of special speeches: *demonstration speeches, speeches of introduction, acceptance speeches,* and *presenting awards.* If your speech is a regular speech, and it fits the basic model we examined in the last two chapters, you may wish to skip this chapter for the time being. You can always refer to it later if you prepare a special speech. If your speech is a special speech, or if you will be giving some other type of unusual speech that isn't listed here, then read on. You will either be able to use the information presented in this chapter or at least adapt your speaking event to one of these four special speeches. So let's get started!

Demonstration Speeches

A **demonstration speech** is a **how-to** speech. It teaches the audience how to do something. Demonstration speeches are different from informative speeches in that the speaker actually shows the audience, step-by-step, the process. Demonstration speaking includes a wide variety of topics and ideas, from simple to complex, such as showing an audience how to make a craft or how to operate a new computer program. Fundamentally, demonstration speeches strive for the following:

1. They present instructions in a step-by-step fashion.
2. They strive to make information easy to understand.
3. They are less formal, sometimes ask ing the audience to try the new task as the speaker guides them.

Demonstration speaking is common in classes, businesses, and specialized clubs such as homemakers clubs, arts and crafts clubs, or gardening clubs. If this sounds like the purpose of your speaking event, let's consider how to write a demonstration speech.

The Model: Demonstration speeches are similar in many ways to the basic speech model, with some important differences.

The basics of a demonstration speech; are:

A. Introduction
B. Transition
C. Body (presented in a step-by-step manner)
D. Transition
E. Conclusion

As you can see, this is similar to the basic speech model, but let's examine each part and look at some examples so that you can see the differences. As with the basic speech model, demonstration speeches are best developed "out of order." If you are writing a demonstration speech, you may want to begin writing the speech in your notebook as we discuss the parts. Let's begin with the body, or the main section of your speech.

1. *The body:* As with a regular speech, you must first decide on your topic and purpose. You probably have this in mind already, but for an example, let's pretend that our speaker, Bob, will be presenting a demonstration speech to a home improvement club that meets once a month. The club focuses on topics and ideas for do-it-yourself home remodeling and landscaping. So, Bob writes his topic and purpose:

```
TOPIC:   How to paint over
         paneling in your home.
PURPOSE: To teach the audience
         how to successfully
         paint over wood
         paneling.
```

Remember that the topic and purpose should be phrased in a one-sentence form. Now that you have your topic and purpose

statements, let's look at the speech body. The major purpose of the speech body is to make the information clear, easy, and orderly so that the audience can follow your instructions. Instead of focusing on major ideas or points, your speech should focus on the steps to complete the process. There are four basic rules:

• Assume that your audience does not know anything about your topic.
• No matter what you talk about, you must provide a demonstration or example of each step.
• Write your speech body in a numbered step format — The first step is ... the second step is ....
• It's a good idea to have no more than ten steps. If you have more steps, your audience will begin to get confused. Five is probably your best number. Your audience can easily remember five steps, but you may have to group steps or information together so that you do not have too many.

Let's begin developing Bob's steps and looking at some important ideas and potential problems. First, always let your first step inform the audience about the supplies and materials they will need for the process. You should have the actual materials on hand to show the audience. Again, do not assume that they know what you are talking about. Bob's speech body would begin like this:

```
   The first step to painting
over paneling in your home is
to gather the supplies you
will need. Of course, you will
need to select the color of
```

```
paint that you desire.  I rec-
ommend an oil-base paint —
latex will tend to peel over
time. You will also need qual-
ity paint primer, a roller
brush, a roller brush pan,
several different sized brush-
es, and fine sandpaper.
```

As Bob begins his speech, he lists the supplies needed, makes a few recommendations, and shows the audience these products. Now he is ready to begin the actual process of demonstrating how to paint paneling. Bob would continue the body of the speech in this manner:

```
    The first step to painting
over paneling in your home is
to gather the supplies you
will need.  Of course, you
will need to select the color
of paint that you desire.  I
recommend an oil-base paint —
latex will tend to peel over
time.  You will also need
quality paint primer, a roller
brush, a roller brush pan,
several different sized brush-
es, and fine sandpaper.
    The second step to success-
fully paint over paneling is
to clean and sand the panel-
ing. Begin by cleaning the
wood....
```

Bob would continue to develop the body of the speech in this step manner as he carefully shows the audience how to paint the paneling. Work on your speech body at this time, structuring it in the step manner that we have examined. As you prepare to write, think about these three important issues and potential problems:

- *A particular problem you should realize as you write is* **dead time.** As you demonstrate how to do something, it is very important that there are no big gaps of silence while you demonstrate a step. In the example above, Bob will have to actually clean and sand a section of the paneling. As he demonstrates the technique, he should carefully explain what to do, but he should also have some back-up material to discuss as he finishes preparing the wood. He might talk about the different kinds of sandpaper or what sandpaper is best for what wood. After you write your speech, it is very important that you practice performing the demonstration so that you can identify dead time sections and be prepared to add extra material.
- *Another important issue is called* **compression of time.** Obviously, there is no way Bob can paint an entire piece of paneling and wait for each coat to dry. So, he will have to demonstrate a step and have a piece of wood already prepared for the next step. This is similar to the cooking shows you see on television. Because of time constraints, they have to speed up the actual time it takes to perform the process for the speech. You will probably have to do the same, depending on the topic.
- *You will have to manage several pieces of equipment to perform a demonstration speech.* Chapter Seven discusses this issue, so follow the basic guidelines given in that chapter.

Once you finish writing the first draft of the speech body, continue to the next section.

2. Introduction: A demonstration speech introduction contains the introductory statements, the main topic or thesis statement, and the number of steps required for the process. It is basically the same as a regular speech introduction as we discussed in Chapter Four, so you should refer to that chapter for more detailed writing tips.

As with a regular speech, you want to begin with a hook — something that catches the audience's attention. You do not want to begin the speech by saying, "Today I'm going to show you how to...." Beginning with a story, a quote, or a joke is a much better choice. Let's return to Bob's speech and develop the introduction for it. Bob decides to begin his speech with a personal story, so he begins his speech like this:

```
A few years ago, a friend
asked me to recommend a good
painter that could paint over
the old paneling in her bed-
room. I said, "Why do you want
to spend your money on labor?
Do the job yourself!" She
replied, "But I can't paint. I
didn't even do well in art when
I was in school. So I don't
think I can paint a room in my
house, can I?"
Well, the truth of the mat-
ter is that my friend could
paint her own house — and she
did! Now I know that you have
all seen pictures of people
happily painting their own
homes, and I also know you have
heard horror stories about
```

```
ruined carpet, uneven brush
strokes, and a huge mess.
```

The speaker begins the speech with a personal story and makes some remarks about the story that relate to the main content. Now that Bob has the audience interested in the subject matter of the speech, he simply adds the next part of the introduction, the main topic or thesis. Essentially, there are two things you want the audience to understand. First, you want the audience to clearly understand what you are going to teach them, and secondly, you want to encourage your audience about the ease of the process. Remember that many people are reluctant and unsure about learning something new, so it's very important that you stress the simplicity of the process you are teaching — even if it isn't very simple! Consider how Bob continues the introduction:

```
A few years ago, a friend
asked me to recommend a good
painter that could paint over
the old paneling in her bed-
room. I said, "Why do you
want to spend your money on
labor? Do the job yourself!"
She replied, "But I can't
paint. I didn't even do well
in art when I was in school.
So I don't think I can paint a
room in my house, can I?"
Well, the truth of the mat-
ter is that my friend could
paint her own house — and she
did! Now I know that you have
all seen pictures of people
```

happily painting their own homes, and I also know you have heard horror stories about ruined carpet, uneven brush strokes, and a huge mess.

Well, painting a paneled room in your home doesn't have to be a nightmare. In fact, it can be very rewarding and even enjoyable if you simply follow a few easy steps. So let's learn how to paint that drab, outdated, paneled room in your home.

Now that Bob has clearly established his topic, he simply needs to add a sentence that tells the audience what is to come in the demonstration. Audiences like to know what to expect, so Bob simply states the number of steps he will show them in his speech. This keeps his audience organized so that they can easily follow him.

A few years ago, a friend asked me to recommend a good painter that could paint over the old paneling in her bedroom. I said, "Why do you want to spend your money on labor? Do the job yourself!" She replied, "But I can't paint. I didn't even do well in art when I was in school. So I don't think I can paint a room in my house, can I?"

Well, the truth of the matter is that my friend could paint her own house — and

she did! Now I know that you have all seen pictures of people happily painting their own homes, and I also know you have heard horror stories about ruined carpet, uneven brush strokes, and a huge mess.

Well. painting a paneled room in your home doesn't have to be a nightmare. In fact, it can be very rewarding and even enjoyable if you simply follow a few easy steps. So let's learn how to paint that drab, outdated, paneled room in your home. Today, you will learn how to paint over paneling in six easy steps.

Now Bob has a complete introduction. It is short and simple, and this is what you want your introduction to look like. Complete your introduction at this time, using Bob's example to guide you.

3. Conclusion: Once your introduction is complete, you are ready to write the conclusion. I recommend that demonstration speech conclusions be very short. You want the audience to mainly remember the steps that you discussed, so once the demonstration is complete, quickly wrap-up the speech.

The demonstration conclusion has two basic parts. First, you want to remind the audience of the number of steps. You probably do not need to give a step summary, but this is acceptable if you feel that it is needed. After you restate the number of steps, end the speech on a positive note that encourages the audience members to try the process on their own. This is Bob's conclusion:

> Today we have learned how to paint a paneled room in six easy steps. As you have seen, you don't have to be a professional painter to remodel a paneled room. You only need a little planning and a little time. So give it a try - you'll be surprised by the difference it will make in your home.

4. Transistions: Once your conclusion is completed, you need to add two final sentences. These are the transitions, or the two sentences that bridge the three main sections of the speech. After your introduction, you need a simple sentence that leads the audience to the body of your speech. Bob's transition from the introduction to the body would simply say, "Before you begin painting a paneled wall, you need to spend a little time planning." This statement leads the audience from general (the introduction) to specifics. The audience knows that Bob is about to actually show them what to do. After the body of your speech, you need a bridge to the conclusion. Again, a simple sentence that takes them out of the step process is all you need. Bob's bridge to his conclusion would say, "Painting a paneled wall is an easy process that any of you can accomplish." This lets his audience know that he is moving away from the steps to the speech conclusion.

As you look back over your speech, you will probably see that it needs some revision. Chapter Six will help you shape up your speech and give you some additional ideas.

One final tip: It's a good idea to let the audience members ask you some questions after you give your speech. This will give them an opportunity to get specific information or ideas from you. Chapter Thirteen discusses question-and-answer sessions in detail.

Speeches of Introduction

A **speech of introduction** is simply a short speech that introduces the main speaker. If you are a member of some organization, perhaps you have been asked to introduce the speaker for the meeting. Speeches of introduction are often not viewed as very important since all they do is introduce the actual speaker. Yet, the speech of introduction is very important to the person you are introducing.

Let's begin by considering the purpose of a speech of introduction. Your fundamental goal is to build credibility and positive feelings about the speaker. This will greatly benefit the speaker and the message he or she is bringing. You want to build these positive feelings, then move aside. There's nothing worse than an introductory speech that is too long and wastes the main speaker's time.

Let's build an introductory speech in a step-by-step format, using Bob once again as our example. Let's say that Bob is introducing Dr. Carla Williams, the speaker at a local service organization in his city. Bob begins the speech by welcoming the audience. This makes the audience feel comfortable and also helps the main speaker. Since Bob is welcoming the audience, Dr. Williams does not have to spend time doing this.

> Good evening! I'm so pleased to see all of you here tonight. Your faithful attendance at our club meetings is commendable.

Now that Bob has welcomed the audience, he begins to introduce the speaker. Your first inclination may be to give the speaker's name, but you should not give the speaker's name until the end of your introduction speech when you ask the audience for applause. Begin by focusing on important background information and the major achievements of the speaker in chronological order. Remember, your purpose is to build credibility and positive feelings about the main speaker. Consider Bob's speech:

> Good evening! I'm so pleased to see all of you here tonight. Your faithful attendance at our club meetings is commendable.
> And you will be glad you're here tonight because you are in for a special treat. Our speaker is certainly no stranger in our community. She received her bachelor's and master's degrees from the University of Alabama, and in 1973, she received a Ph.D. in child development from the University of California. A few short years later, she

became the director of Clanton Child Home here in our city. Since that time, this orphanage has become one of the best homes in the United States. Our speaker has won numerous national awards for her work, and most importantly, she has made a positive impact in the lives of thousands of children.

As in the example above, you want to point out the speaker's credentials and briefly comment on the speaker's accomplishments. Next, add the final sentence, stating the speaker's name and asking the audience for applause.

> Good evening! I'm so pleased to see all of you here tonight. Your faithful attendance at our club meetings is commendable. And you will be glad you're here tonight because you are in for a special treat. Our speaker is certainly no stranger in our community. She received her bachelor's and master's degrees from the University of Alabama, and in 1973, she received a Ph.D. in child development from the University of California. A few short years later, she became the director of Clanton Child Home here in our city. Since that time, this orphanage has become one of the best homes in the United States.

```
Our speaker has won numerous
national awards for her work,
and most importantly, she has
made a positive impact in the
lives of thousands of chil-
dren.
     Please join me in giving a
warm welcome to Dr. Carla
Williams.
```

Once you complete your sentence, begin the applause and remain at the podium until the speaker arrives. Once the speaker is at the podium, shake hands with the speaker and move quickly to your chair.

Remember, your purpose is to build positive feelings for the main speaker. Do not use the introductory speech for any other purpose, and keep it short. A speech of introduction should not be longer than a minute and a half.

Acceptance Speeches

Acceptance speeches cover a variety of occasions from accepting a position to an award of some kind. Depending on the type of acceptance speech you will give, you will have to adapt the following basic guidelines to your needs. There are, however, some very important ideas for successful acceptance speaking. Consider these points:

- An acceptance speech is a time to thank people who have helped you. It is not a time to discuss your achievements or even your future goals. If you have been awarded a leadership position in your club or business, you might need to give a brief acceptance speech, then discuss your leadership goals. If you have been given an award, and you are the keynote speaker for the event, then give a brief acceptance speech before you move to your main speech. If you need to do this, follow the basic speech model in Chapters Three and Four.
- Spend your time focusing on how much the award means to you. Do not spend your time playing on humility by saying, "I really don't deserve this, but...."
- Be gracious and modest.
- Keep it short.

As an example, let's pretend that our speaker, Bob has been given the "businessperson of the year" award by the local chamber of commerce. He is presented the award at a banquet where he is not the keynote speaker. So, he gives the following speech:

```
     I can't tell you how
thrilled I am to accept this
award this evening. When I
was first informed that I was
to receive this year's "busi-
nessperson of the year" award,
I was quite surprised consid-
ering all of the fine business
people we have in our city. I
am so thankful to be an active
part in our city's economic
success.
     But my personal success is
due to many other people. I
would like to thank my family
for their constant support and
willingness to work right
```

along with me. I would also
like to thank you, my friends
in the business community, for
your sound advice and help
during the past several years.
I have to include you in the
success of my business because
so many of you have helped so
much.

Finally, I would like to
thank you for your belief in
me, and I hope to continue
to have a positive impact in
our city for years to come.
Thank you for this award — I
consider it a great honor.

Notice that the primary purpose of the speech is to thank the people who have helped him and to put the spotlight back on the audience members. This is a very gracious way to accept an award and one that will create very positive feelings.

Presenting an Award

Finally, special speeches include presenting an award to another person. If you are asked to present an award, follow the same guidelines as a speech of introduction. Basically, you want to build credibility and positive feelings before you give the award to the person. Let's say that Bob returns the next year to present the "businessperson of the year" award to another person. Consider Bob's presentation:

It is my pleasure to pre-
sent the "businessperson of
the year" award, and the person who will receive this
award tonight is certainly
deserving.

In 1956, he opened a small
corner store in the downtown
section that sold cattle and
horse feed as well as animal
husbandry supplies. Two years
later, he began creating and
selling his own grooming
equipment especially for show
horses. Since that modest
beginning, his business has
grown, developing over fifty
patents and employing over two
hundred people who manufacture
and sell the internationally
recognized Frankston Horse
Products.

Please join me in welcoming
this year's "businessperson of
the year," John Frankston.

As with a speech of introduction, you want to avoid giving the person's name until the end of the speech, and make sure you invite the audience to applaud the award winner.

This chapter has focused on four special speeches. Remember that if your speaking event does not exactly match the four types discussed, you can still adapt your speech to the models and examples given. Just remember to follow the basic guidelines while keeping your speech purpose in mind at all times.

Now move to the next chapter and let's turn the rough draft of your speech into a great piece of work!

Creating Your Final Draft

First drafts are a lot like first loves — they are usually not the best for you! As I worked on this book, several friends said, "Writing a book must be difficult." I would always say, "Writing a book is easy; editing a book is extremely difficult." The same can be said for your speech. You have your first draft completed, and now we need to turn your first draft into a first-rate speech. This is called editing. We often think of editing as cutting out wording or information, but actually, we should think of editing as "reworking and adding."

Through the next several pages, we are going to work on a wide variety of writing techniques that will transform your rough draft into a final draft. This chapter is divided into two major parts, editing and style, that contain sections which discuss a wide range of topics. After you read each section, stop and work on your speech, then move on to the next section. This way, you will be editing your speech while focusing on only one item instead of trying to edit several concepts at one time.

I strongly recommend that you read out loud. Listen to the way the speech sounds as you say it and make changes according to what sounds best. Also, rereading and working on your speech will help you get familiar with the text. So get your pen ready!

Before we get started, you should understand a major component of an effective final draft — **conversational tone.** Conversational tone is simply communication that sounds like a conversation between people. Basically, you want to talk "to" your audience — not "at" them. Writing a speech that sounds conversational is primarily accomplished through sentence structure and vocabulary usage. So let's spend some time working on these in Part One.

Part One: Editing

When you worked on your speech in Chapters Three, Four, and Five, you probably noticed that your speech seemed boring or "flat." In this section, we are going to work on your speech, adding some information and possibly reworking part of it to make your speech more interesting and effective.

Sentence Structure: No, you're not sitting in English class again, but there are some major ideas we should consider so that your speech will be well written and have a natural flow.

1. *Sentence Fragments:* A **sentence fragment,** for the most part, is simply a sentence that is incomplete — it lacks either a subject, verb, or possibly both. Although fragments are not appropriate in most written communication, they may serve a useful purpose in a speech. Read this section:

> As we work from day to day in our various occupations, we should all strive for excellence. After all, excellence is the most important key to a successful business. The most important.

Obviously, the last sentence is a fragment, yet the fragment serves the purpose of emphasizing a major idea in the speech. Reread the sentence out loud. You will notice that the statement could be effective, depending on how the speaker presents it. Generally, avoid fragments when giving a speech unless the fragment serves some specific delivery purpose. Review your speech at this time, correcting sentence fragments or possibly adding a few here and there if they will make your speech more effective. Again, read the speech out loud as you edit.

2. *Run-On Sentences:* **Run-on sentences** are simply what the name suggests — sentences that seem to never end. Consider this sentence:

> One of the greatest resources any of us can ever hope to have is human resources because the skill, vitality, energy, and creativeness of human beings is something that we all need in our occupations, our homes, our personal lives, and our recreation time since we all live in the same world and depend upon one another for various needs and desires each day as we go about our business, and these resources are so necessary that the possibility of success without others seems quite bleak and...

See what I mean? Not only is this sentence very irritating, it is also very tiring. Remember that each audience member must mentally process the information that you are presenting in your speech, and long, complex sentences are one sure way to make your audience begin to daydream and tune you out. This does not mean that each sentence in your speech should be simple and elementary. You need a wide variety of sentence structures to make your speech interesting, but you never want to use a run-on

Chapter 6: Creating Your Final Draft 55

sentence. Edit your script at this time and correct any run-on or overly complex sentence construction.

3. *Redundant Construction:* Another sentence problem that can creep into your speech is **redundant construction.** This common problem is simply sentences, phrases, or words that unnecessarily repeat an idea. Let's look at some examples.

• "Voting is extremely important for each American. We must vote. Each person in this room today has a responsibility to vote during this campaign." As you can see, these sentences say the same thing. One sentence is sufficient.

• "During this campaign, as we work together before the election, while we have a chance to bring about change, I ask for your help." This is a good example of phrase redundancy. The opening phrases say the same thing over and over, and one of these is enough.

• "It is positively, absolutely, unequivocally, and without a doubt necessary for you to vote." This is a good example of word redundancy. One of the repeating words would have conveyed to the audience the meaning of the sentence, but all of the words strung together seem to give it somewhat of a comic appeal.

At times, a redundant sentence, phrase, or word may be used for effect and delivery purposes, but as a general rule, avoid redundancy unless you have a specific purpose in mind.

4. *Passive Voice:* In most sentences, the subject should perform the action of the verb. A sentence in which the action is not performed by the subject is called **passive voice.** Consider the following example:

The speaker inspired the audience.

This sentence is written in the active voice. The subject (speaker) performs an action (inspiring) to a direct object (audience). Now read this sentence:

The audience was inspired by the speaker.

This sentence is written in the passive voice. The subject is still "the speaker," but the direct object (audience) is performing the action (being inspired).

Passive voice sentences always contain a verb phrase consisting of some form of *be* (is, was, were, be, been, being, etc.) and a past participle such as *will speak, is speaking, were speaking, etc.*

In general, passive voice is not a grammatical error, however, try to speak mostly in the active voice. Your speech will sound more interesting and be more "action" oriented.

Vocabulary: Now let's look at three major ideas that relate to vocabulary that will further develop conversational tone. Again, make sure you read your speech out loud as you work through each section.

1. *Complex Vocabulary:* Overly **complex vocabulary** is a great communication barrier. If you made a perfect score on the verbal section of the Scholastic Aptitude Test (SAT), a speech is not the time to show off your skills, I am sorry to say. Consider this example:

Although the complexity and obtrusive nature of existence can be inherently intimidating and speculative, we must contend to execute the incomparable every waking moment.

What does it say? Translation:

Life is uncertain and difficult, but we must try to do our best each day.

As you can see, the second sentence easily communicates while the first one may leave the audience wondering what was said. Now imagine an entire speech written in the style of the first example. The audience would be quickly lost, which is not what you want. Remember that the definition of communication is sending an understandable message.

Of course, you do not want to "talk down" to your audience, but you also do not want to tax their brains any more than necessary! Obviously, the style of vocabulary you choose to use may depend on the situation and your audience. Just remember, as we already noted in Chapter One, the only reason for giving a speech is to communicate with a group of people. Make sure the vocabulary can be easily understood by everyone in your audience. Even if you are speaking to an "academic" audience — be careful. Reread your speech and analyze the vocabulary you have used. Rewrite any sections that seem too advanced or too simple, and keep your audience in mind as you do this.

2. *Gender and Racial Bias:* **Gender and racial bias** is another problem that will hinder you in creating a positive, conversational speech to convince your audience. Generally, gender and racial bias is easy to avoid — just make sure that none of your statements contain any degrading or inappropriate remarks regarding race or gender. Another important point that may directly impact your wording is pronoun usage. Make sure that all of your pronouns are not worded in the masculine (he) form. A combination of he/she wording is best. For example:

Every public speaker should do his or her best.

This sentence is not gender biased since it refers to both sexes. Also be careful with words like "salesman," "statesman," "policeman," etc. Try to use words like "salesperson," "statesperson," etc. Of course, you do not have to be so politically correct that your speech begins to sound ridiculous, but watch for words or phrases that may be viewed as gender or racially biased.

3. *Inclusive Pronouns:* **Inclusive pronouns** are simply words that include your audience in your speech, and this is one of the most important skills to create conversational tone. Inclusive pronouns will make your speech sound like you are talking with your audience. Read this example:

This speech will examine some common problems in computer literacy.

Now read this example that uses inclusive pronouns:

> **Let's talk about some common problems in computer literacy.**

See the difference? The first example refers to the actual speech while the second example focuses on the audience. Inclusive pronouns are a major way to give your speech a conversational tone and include your audience in your presentation. This is the same approach I have taken in writing this book. You have probably noticed that I regularly make statements like "let's discuss," "let's look at," "let's think about," as well as others. This is the approach you want to take. Instead of talking to your audience — talk with them. Obviously, you are the only one talking, just as I am the only one writing, but you want your audience to feel like they are included.

I attended a concert several years ago in a large coliseum in Houston. About 15,000 people attended this concert, but when the singer talked to us, I felt like we were sitting around her living room having a conversation. The conversation was warm, friendly, and personal. This is what you want for your speech. Reread your speech and change any "I will talk to you about..." statements to include your audience. Also, does your speech generally sound like you are simply talking to other people? If not, strive for a more conversational tone between you and your audience.

Using Examples: Examples are very important in both writing and speaking. Basically, examples provide meaning and understanding for concepts or ideas that you present in your speech. There are three basic types of examples, and your speech text should be full of these. You will probably add quite a bit of material to your speech as you work on this section, so you may want to read the following sections discussing the types of examples before you begin editing your speech. Remember, see Appendix A for two sample speeches that you may use as models.

1. *Supporting Examples:* **Supporting examples** describe or further explain some idea or concept. In other words, they help the audience understand what you are talking about, and they keep the audience interested in the content of your speech. This section from a speech contains a supporting example:

> **The epiglottis is a triangular flap of cartilage that covers the entrance to the wind pipe. It keeps food from traveling into the lungs. The epiglottis works a lot like a valve on a water faucet — at just the right time, it closes the area, preventing matter from passing through.**

As you can see, the example helps the audience understand the content and makes the content more meaningful and interesting. Your speech should use many supporting examples. Look back over your audience analysis notes and try to use examples that relate to the major "connecting areas" that you discovered.

2. *Qualifying Examples:* **Qualifying examples** qualify, or make significant, statements or content in your speech. They are normally used to support research, facts, or statistical information and make the information more relevant and memorable. Consider this statement:

> **The Voyager 2 spacecraft used each planet's gravitational field to help move itself onto its next destination—at just over 61,000 miles per hour.**

There is nothing wrong with this statement, and it provides interesting information. However, just how fast is 61,000 miles per hour? We know it's fast, but how fast? Let's add a qualifying example to the sentence.

> **The Voyager 2 spacecraft used each planet's gravitational field to help move itself onto its next destination—at just over 61,000 miles per hour. That's twenty times faster than a speeding bullet!**

The qualifying statement puts the 61,000 miles per hour in a different light. It's hard to visualize 61,000 miles per hour, but when we realize that this speed is twenty times faster than a speeding bullet, *Voyager 2's* speed is astonishing. Qualifying examples will help your audience understand incredible facts or statistics you are using in your speech. Here's another example.

> **So many Americans are hooked on playing the lottery, even though the odds against winning are 1 in 16 million. Of course, those odds don't sound too bad, until you realize that you are more likely to be in five airplane crashes or be struck by lightning eight times!**

Again, the qualifying examples put the "1 in 16 million" in a different light. The odds of winning the lottery are so great that they almost have no meaning, but the qualifying examples help the audience truly understand the odds. Check your speech for facts or statistics that can be enhanced by using qualifying examples. You may have to search a little to find the information to use as a qualifying example, but the results will be well worth it.

3. *Personal Testimony:* **Personal testimony** can be very useful in a speech. For the most part, personal testimonies are "examples" in that they back up some information or ideas that you have already presented. There are, however, two basic rules you should follow if you decide to use a personal testimony.

First, make sure that the testimony is true. In other words, do not talk about your experiences on the ski slope if you have never been skiing. Second, keep it short and think carefully about why you are using the testimony. Make sure that the testimony directly builds your speech topic and focus and is not just stuck in for the sake of telling a story about yourself. Again, keep the focus of the speech on the topic.

Logical Fallacies: Logical fallacies are simply logic errors. In other words, they are statements that are simply untrue and also unreasonable. You may think that you have no logic errors in your speech and be tempted to skip over this section, but don't! They can appear in your writing, and you might not even realize it. Let's look at some common types, and check over your speech as you read to make sure you have not used any of these.

1. *Card Stacking:* **Card stacking** is presenting only the information that backs up an idea and not all of the information that is relevant. For example, let's say that you are a milk salesperson asked to give a speech about milk. You are guilty of card stacking if you tell the audience how good milk is for them, but fail to tell the audience about the calories and fat in each glass as well as the fact that too much milk will cause weight gain. Again, no matter what you are talking about, be honest.

2. *Bandwagon:* **Bandwagon** is stating that everyone believes in a certain idea or concept. For example, a speaker may tell his or her audience that all Americans love dogs, when in fact, all Americans do not love dogs.

3. *Hasty Generalization:* **Hasty generalization** is the very common fallacy of placing people into certain groups who act in a certain way — or stereotyping people. For example, the statement "All Texans wear cowboy hats" is an example of hasty generalization.

4. *Glittering Generality:* **Glittering generality** is using a word or phrase that is so vague that no one really knows what it means. For example, a politician may say that he or she is in favor of freedom of speech, but how does the politician actually define freedom of speech? Be sure that you define any overly broad terms so that the audience members do not interpret the idea in a way that you do not intend.

5. *Testimonial:* A **testimonial** is the opinion of some famous person on a particular subject. This should not be confused with personal testimony. Testimonials are basically opinions from people who are not experts on the subject. For example, an actor may perform a commercial advertising a pain medication. Although the actor may capture the audience's attention, the actor probably does not have expert knowledge about medications. Make sure that any person you quote is an expert on the subject matter.

Part Two: Style

So far, we have worked on a number of editing issues as we turn your rough draft into a final draft. At this point, we will begin to work on some style techniques to dress up some sections of your speech. Some of the ideas presented on the following pages may overlap or ask you to further develop some of the editing problems we worked on in Part One. Again, this part of speech development is very tiring, but continue to work on each section and read your speech out loud as you work on style. I promise, this will help you.

English Usage: Let's focus first on some style issues related to vocabulary that can impact your speech in a positive way if used correctly. Most of the topics will further develop conversational tone as we discussed in Part One.

1. *Jargon:* **Jargon** is an advanced level of technical language found primarily in certain occupations or businesses. Although jargon is not inappropriate, it may confuse your audience if it is not familiar with the jargon. Consider this example:

> A three-factor multivariate analysis of variance was performed to determine whether there was a difference in effects of category, gender, and teaching field on the multivariate response variable attitude toward kinesics.

This example of jargon discusses a statistical technique used in research analysis. Although there is nothing wrong with the statement, the speaker should question whether or not all audience members will understand it. If this speaker was talking to a group of statisticians, the sentence would be fine, but if the speaker was not, the jargon should be avoided. There are many occupations that use jargon, especially the medical, computer, engineering, and business fields. The main point to remember is that your audience must be able to understand you. Check back over your speech at this time, correcting any jargon that is too technical or unclear as you keep your audience in mind.

2. *Slang:* **Slang** is very informal language that we all use to some extent when we speak to each other. Although slang is usually not appropriate in most written communication, it can be used sparingly in a speech, if you are sure that your audience will understand and not be turned off by the slang that you use. Remember that slang tends to be regional — meaning that slang used by people who live in Texas may not be used by people who live in New York. If you are speaking to a group of people from your geographic location, then some slang wording is fine and will make you seem more approachable, but if you are speaking to a diverse group of people, avoid slang wording. Sometimes people perceive the use of slang to be uneducated, so be careful about the image you project by your word choices. Review your speech at this time, editing or adding slang language if it is appropriate for your audience.

3. *Colloquialisms:* **Colloquialisms** are terms or phrases that are used in conversation but are not considered formal language. Some common examples are: "He was down in the mouth," "It was an underhanded deal," and "You should let sleeping dogs lie." Colloquialisms tend to be regional and may not communicate clearly with all audience members, so you should avoid them.

4. *Cliches:* **Cliches** are phrases that have been used so often that they are no longer effective. Some examples are "over the hill" and "pretty as a picture." This is one aspect of style that you want to avoid. Search for phrases or wording that is more original and avoid overly-used phrases or expressions.

5. *Euphemisms:* **Euphemisms** are words or phrases that replace some unpleasant words or phrases. For example, a speaker may say, "We had to put our cat to sleep," instead of using the word "kill." Euphemisms are important and are often used for the purposes of good taste, but be careful not to over use them - be as direct as possible.

6. *Denotation – Connotation:* **Denotation** is the exact definition of a word while **connotation** is a slang or understood meaning. For example, the denotative meaning of "cool" has to do with temperature, while the connotative meaning may have to do with a person's attitude, demeanor, or style. The point to remember for your speech is that each audience member should get the same meaning from the words you choose, so be careful of the connotative meanings some words may carry that may cause unintentional communication or miscommunication.

Using Humor: Humor is a major part of all of our lives. From our conversations, to what we read, to movies and television, humor is something we all enjoy. And certainly, humor can greatly build a speech. But humor is not easy to write and can devastate a speaking situation if the audience does not respond. Let's look at some basic guidelines for using humor in your speech.

1. *Any humor you use must directly build your speech topic or illustrate some idea or example.* Never use humor just to get a laugh.

2. *Humor must always be appropriate.* As stated in Chapter One, no matter what the occasion or audience, racially or gender degrading humor is not appropriate. Additionally, avoid jokes or stories that use profanity, sexually oriented material, or sexual innuendoes. You are better off to stay on the safe side than take the chance of alienating your audience.

3. *Make sure the humor sounds conversational.* In other words, you may need to rewrite the joke slightly to make it fit your particular style of speaking.

4. *Humor needs to be fresh.* Avoid any jokes, puns, or stories that are frequently used.

5. *Keep it short and to the point.* Most jokes that take a long time to tell aren't funny.

As you think about adding humor to your speech, keep in mind that there are a number of resources available to you. Most bookstores have paperback books which contain jokes and funny stories for speakers and writers. The Resource section at the end of this book suggests several resources you can refer to. You may want to use one of these resources. Finally, always try humor out on some friends or family members before you put it in the speech. This way, you can get some feedback about whether or not a joke is funny before you try it out on an audience.

Making Your Speech Memorable: Why do some speeches seem to stand the test of time while others fade? Why do some speeches seem to inspire and motivate people while a similar speech about the same subject does nothing? The answer, aside from a wel-developed topic and support material, is in phrasing. Consider John F. Kennedy's, "Ask not what your country can do for you, ask what you can do for your country," or Martin Luther King's "I have a dream" phrases. These speeches are primarily remembered because of content and effective phrasing. Speech phrasing is sometimes called "rhetorical technique," and we will look at some major ways you can emphasize some of your most important ideas. You might want to read over this entire section before you work on your speech so you will be able to target certain changes or rewrites for some of your sentences.

1. *Imagery:* **Imagery** is writing that uses words which appeal to the five senses and create mental images. In other words, imagery helps your audience "see" what you are talking about instead of just hearing what you are talking about. Consider this sentence:

```
When I went swimming, the
water was cold.
```

Now read this example which uses imagery:

```
When I went swimming, the
icy water felt like a million
bees stinging my skin.
```

This example contains the same basic information as the first sentence, however, words like "icy" and "stinging" create mental images because they appeal to the senses. Also, this sentence uses a simile — a comparison that uses "like" or "as." "Like a million bees" compares the feeling of the cold water to a bee sting, thus creating a mental image for the audience. As you work on your speech, watch for descriptive sections that can be enhanced by using imagery. As you work on these sections, think of sensory words — this will help you dress up some of your phrases.

Be careful that you do not overuse imagery techniques. This is sometimes called "flowery wording." Consider this example:

```
As we walked down the lonely
road, we noticed some tangled
vines hanging from the   trees
like large ropes before us.
The texture of the vines felt
like soft rubber which was
```

```
delicate to touch.  I noticed
that the vines felt very old
and worn, such as a garment
that has been in storage....
```

Now imagine an entire speech written like this. Imagery is a vital technique that can enhance your speech, but a little goes a long way. Remember to stay focused on your topic and get to the point. If you begin to use imagery in some sections, ask yourself these questions so that you avoid flowery wording:

• Does the section that uses imagery directly build my speech topic? In other words, is this a major idea or example I want my audience to remember?

• Am I using imagery consistently in every section or example? If you are, you are probably overdoing it. Read your speech out loud. Does it sound like conversation, or does it sound like you are trying to win a poetry contest?

2. *Parallel Structure:* **Parallel structure** is another technique that can create memorable phrases. Basically, parallel structure groups words or phrases that "copy" or echo each other for emphasis and impact. Read this example:

```
It is now time for our
nation to rise up against
crime.  It is now time for us
to rise up against crime.
```

The second sentence copies the first in that it has the same content, but it is different because it reiterates the statement to make it personal for the audience. Again, this technique enables the speaker to emphasize a major idea or point.

3. *Antithesis:* **Antithesis** is like parallel structure, except the copying word or phrase is directly opposite in meaning. This technique creates "conflict" between the two words or phrases to heighten the meaning. Consider this example:

> **This was the best campaign ever — and the worst.**

This example creates a direct contrast in meaning, and this statement enables the speaker to begin comparing the positive and negative aspects of the campaign. Both parallel structure and antithesis are effective techniques, but again, use them sparingly. Remember to only use these techniques on points or sections that are most important for your audience to remember.

4. *Interruption:* Another technique which can be used to emphasize important points is **interruption.** Interruption is simply the use of a "built-in" pause. Read this example out loud:

> **Jupiter's "red spot" is actually just a hole in an extremely stormy atmosphere. However, the planet is so large that this single red spot is about three times the size of Earth!**

Now read this example again. When you come to the dash (—), pause for a brief moment, then read the rest.

> **Jupiter's "red spot" is actually just a hole in an extremely stormy atmosphere. However, the planet is so large that this single red spot is about — three times the size of Earth!**

See the difference? The interruption creates anticipation and builds emphasis for this qualifying example. Again, interruptions are important and can be used to emphasize important points or information, but do not over use them.

5. *Hyperbole:* **Hyperbole** is a technique that uses extreme exaggeration that is not meant to be taken literally. Often, a hyperbole is used to give a point or example a comic or light-hearted appeal. This is a common example:

> **This headache is killing me!**

Obviously, if you use this statement, no one expects you to die, but the emphasis is understood. Here's another example:

> **The class lasted for an eternity.**

Again, the class didn't last an "eternity," but the statement is used for emphasis. Use this technique to convey a major point or idea, and do not use a hyperbole unless you have a specific purpose in mind.

6. *Repetition:* The last technique that can enhance some of your phrases is **repetition.** Repeating words, phrases, or ideas is a good way to create effective statements and also to keep your audience organized and interested in the topic. Consider Abraham Lincoln's phrase from the Gettysburg Address:

```
"...that government of the
people, by the people, and for
the people..."
```

In this phrase, Lincoln repeats "the people" for emphasis — "the people" are the government. As you think about your speech, be careful when using repeating words or phrases — some words or phrases simply do not sound good, so always say your speech out loud as you work on it.

Remember that well-constructed, effective phrases create a speech that people will remember. Use some of these techniques to emphasize major ideas or statements in your speech text.

This chapter has focused on editing and style. By now, you should have a speech that is nearing completion. Once again, I recommend that you read your speech out loud and look for any areas that need improvement. You may want someone to listen to you as you read and offer suggestions or point out areas that seem unclear. It is probably best if you do not let someone read your speech — he or she will get a better understanding of your style if they hear it. As you edit your speech for the last time, keep the following major ideas in mind. You should be able to answer "yes" to these questions:

- **Is your speech conversational? As you read out loud, does your speech sound like you are talking "with" people?**

- **Does your speech include your audience? Are your examples and support material relevant to your audience? (See your audience analysis notes if not.) Have you used inclusive statements such as "let's talk about" or "we will consider," etc.?**

- **Have you tried to enhance your major ideas by using "rhetorical techniques?"**

- **Are you personally comfortable with the language and style of your speech?**

Congratulations! You have finished your speech. The next several chapters will teach you how to present it to your audience!

CHAPTER SEVEN

Using Visual Aids

A picture is not always worth a thousand words! The use of visual aids can greatly enhance a speech, or greatly damage its effectiveness. This chapter discusses different types of visual aids and how to use them in your speech. You may not have considered using visual aids, but they can be great speech builders. Before you begin practicing your speech, you should consider the possibility of using visual aids. Let's look at the basic purpose of visual aids in a speaking situation.

As discussed in Chapter One, a message travels through channels, which are our five senses. In a speaking situation, the message primarily travels through sound. Some visual communication is included because the audience can see the speaker, and the speaker's expressions and gestures help convey the message. But sometimes the content of a speech needs some additional help to be understood by an audience — and this is the purpose of visual aids. Basically, a visual aid is something your audience can see that aids or helps your speech content. Visual aids may be used to support examples, major ideas or points, or factual content. For example, if a speaker

was discussing the shape and structure of the atom, a picture or slide of the atom would greatly help the audience understand the speech content.

Visual aids should always support the speech content, *not the other way around.* In other words, the visual aid should be a natural extension of the speech, and the speech should not be built around various media products. You have probably seen a speech that consisted of a series of overhead transparencies with the speaker making a few comments on each transparency — this is not an effective speech.

This chapter is divided into three major sections: *types of visual aids, creating visual aids,* and *methods of presentation.* Before we examine the major types of visual aids, let's consider some basic guidelines for visual aid usage. You can apply these guidelines to every type of visual aid.

1. *Visual aids must support the speech.* Don't show a picture for the sake of showing a picture.

2. *Visual aids must be relevant.* In other words, the visual aids you use should exist to help the audience understand the message. Let's say you are giving a speech

about the nutrition of fast food. You probably do not need to show your audience pictures of pizza and french fries, since your audience members have all seen these items. The visual aid needs to show us something new — something we do not already know.

3. *No matter what visual aid you use, only allow the audience to see the visual aid when it is being discussed.* In other words, hide the visual aid once you are finished talking about it. For example, if you show the audience a chart, discuss the chart, then hide it before you move on to the next section of your speech. This way, your audience will not continue to look at the visual aid while you are talking about something else. This will help keep the audience focused on the speech content. This idea will be explained in more detail as we discuss types of equipment.

4. *Always keep it simple.* Do not overload your audience with information.

5. *Always look at and talk to the audience, not the visual aid.* This idea will be discussed further in Chapter Nine.

6. *Make sure you are comfortable using the visual aid.* Do not try to use something that makes you uncomfortable.

These basic guidelines will help you make decisions about your media needs. Keep these basics in mind constantly as you read the rest of the chapter.

Common Types of Visual Aids

Now let's go into a little more detail and discuss the strengths, weaknesses, and special problems of some types of visual aids used in public speaking. As you read, think about your speech content and what kind of visual aids might be best for your speech.

Graphs: Graphs normally illustrate numerical or statistical information and are commonly used in speeches. Graphs generally enable the audience to quickly understand information that would be difficult to comprehend if the speaker only used verbal communication.

There are three basic types of graphs: pie, line, and bar.

- Pie graphs are used to present parts of a whole such as statistical information, sale information, or expenditures. For example, let's say that a company spokesperson is giving a speech about company expenditures. If the speaker states that the office supply expenses make up 24.8% of the expense budget, the statistic may not seem significant without a graph illustration, such as the one shown in Figure 11. This sample pie graph is effective and could be enlarged to any size or adapted for any purpose.

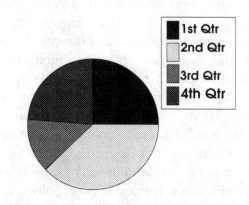

Figure 11. *Pie graph*

- Line graphs (Figure 12) are another effective type of graph used to present specific high and low points. Line graphs are particularly useful because the speaker can point to difference sections while discussing the content. Line graphs are most effective to demonstrate change over a period of time. They can be used to show sales figures, expenditures, or percentage changes such as a rise in expenses.

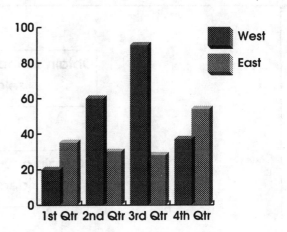

Figure 13. *Bar graph*

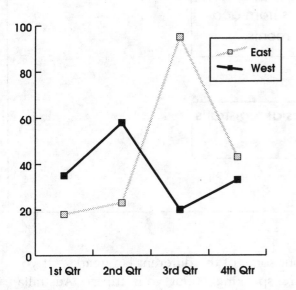

Figure 12. *Line graph*

- Bar graphs (Figure 13) are particularly suited to compare two or more figures or sets of figures. Bar graphs are used to present the same information as a line graph, but bar graphs can compare two or more sets of data and keep the audience organized amid all of the facts.

Pie, line, and bar graphs are all effective, but there are a few points to remember: Color graphs are effective, just be careful not to combine dark colors. Also, make sure that your numbers or percentages will be large enough for your audience to see. Finally, keep it simple. Do not try to include every possible piece of information — create several graphs instead of including all of the information on one.

Charts: Charts are generally drawings that show relationships or the steps of a process. Charts usually contain graphics and wording and can be used for almost any subject. Let's say that a college registrar is giving a speech to a group of freshman students who are about to register for courses. The speaker might use a chart like the one in Figure 14.

Although this information is not difficult to understand, the speaker is talking about a series of steps the audience members must follow. This chart will help the students remember what to do for registration, and they can even copy it if they so desire.

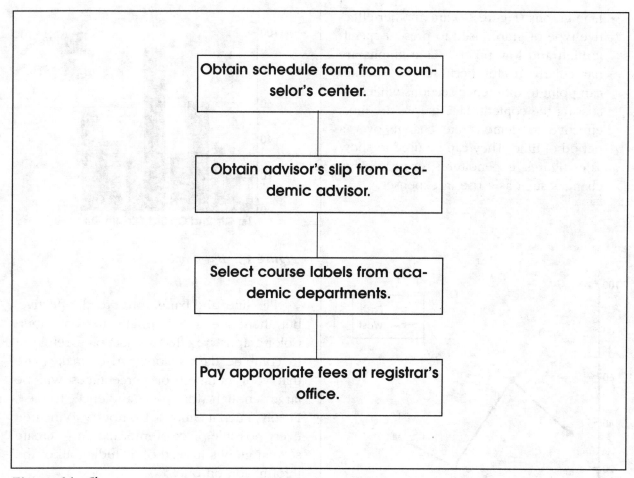

Figure 14. *Chart*

Overall, charts are very effective, but the same rules for using a graph apply — keep it simple, to the point, and only show the audience the chart as you are speaking about the content.

Maps: Maps are another type of visual aid that can be effective. There are a few simple points to keep in mind when using a map. First, only use a map if your audience is unaware of a particular location you are discussing. For example, if you are talking about your recent trip to Shakespeare's home, you might want to use a map to point out some of the different landmarks. If you are speaking about your trip to Australia, you could use a map to locate some of the different areas you visited, but you would not need to show the audience the location of Australia on the globe since most of your audience would probably already know that information. Again, only use a visual aid to show the audience something that it might not understand with only your verbal communication.

Pictures: Pictures are a commonly used type of visual aid. "Pictures" include posters, drawings, paintings, and photographs. Any of these can be used to support your speech material.

- Posters and drawings are effective and very useful since you can combine a picture of some kind with lettering. However, all lettering and pictures you use must be large enough for the audience to see. You may have seen a speaker hold up a photo and say something like, "I know all of you can't see this, but....". This is not what you want to do. All audience members must be able to easily see the picture, so think carefully about your speaking situation before you use this type of visual aid. Again, do not overcrowd a poster or drawing — keep it simple so the audience can easily see it.

- Paintings and photographs are useful if they are relevant and directly aid your speech. For example, if you are giving a speech about antique cars, pictures of the automobiles are certainly appropriate and useful. The problem with paintings and photographs is size. You must make sure that your audience members will be able to see them.

  Another special problem with paintings and photographs is glare. Depending on the lighting in the room in which you are speaking, paintings and photos will usually glare at certain angles, thus making the picture impossible for some audience members to see. If you decide to use a painting or a photo, be sure to inspect the room before you speak so that you will be able to compensate for any lighting problems.

Cartoons: Cartoons can add humor to visual aids or create satire to make a point. They are particularly effective if you are trying to add a touch of humor to a serious subject. Several years ago, I delivered a speech about three common snakes and the myths about those snakes. Pictures of the myths were painted in a cartoon style, thus making the myths funny. Then I presented actual photographs of the snakes. The cartoon with the actual photo helped further convey the message of myth verses reality. If you use a cartoon, make sure it is large enough, contains enough color, and actually has a purpose in aiding your speech. Never use a cartoon just for the sake of adding humor to the speech.

Film: Film or tape clips can add an effective dimension to a speech. A particular use for film clips is "sequence events." Let's say, for example, that a doctor is giving a speech about a surgical process to a group of medical students. To help the students fully understand the process, film footage that shows this process would certainly be effective. As with all other visual aids, make sure that the film directly supports or aids the speech topic — and keep it short.

Handouts: A handout is something prepared ahead of time to give to each audience member. It may contain an outline, a map, a chart, or other materials. The purpose of a handout is to give the audience something they can refer to once the speech is finished. However, handouts do pose a particular problem because once the speaker gives them to the audience, he or she cannot control them. Since you do not want your audience looking at the handout while you are speaking, the best way to use handouts is to give them to the audience after the speech.

If you do plan to give the audience members a handout after the speech, do not end your speech by saying, "At this time I will provide you with a handout." Remember that your concluding sentences are some of your most important, and you do not want your audience to mainly remember that you gave them a handout. When you come to the section of your speech that discusses the handout, simply tell the audience that you will provide them with a handout after the speech. For example, let's say you are giving a speech about automobile safety. While you are talking about the steps of safe driving, simply tell the audience members that you will give them a handout that contains the steps at the end of the speech, then move on and do not mention it again during the speech.

Objects: Sometimes, a speaker may want to use something that is three dimensional to aid the audience in understanding the speech content. Objects are appropriate in most speaking situations, if all of the audience members are able to see them. For example, let's say that a geologist is speaking to an audience about some common types of minerals. The speaker would probably want to have samples of the minerals to use as visual aids during the speech and for the audience to examine once the speech is over.

Models: Models can be used in both picture and object form. They are especially useful if you are demonstrating how something works. For example, if a speaker is explaining how an engine works, he or she might want to use a model of some kind that would make the speech content easier to understand. Make sure that any model is simple and contains only the parts that you plan to discuss in your speech.

Special Speech Aids: For some specialized speeches, a twist on visual aids is needed. Let's say that a speaker is discussing the work of Beethoven. The speaker might need a sound aid - sounds that help the audience understand the content. The speaker might want to play some samples of Beethoven's music during certain sections of the speech. Or, if a speaker is discussing the three most popular brands of perfume, he or she might need smell aids — samples of the scents for the audience. Virtually anything can be an effective visual aid!

Obviously, these are not the only possible types of visual aids — almost anything that will aid your speech content can be used. Just keep the basic guidelines in mind constantly if you decide to use media. Now that we have examined some of the fundamental types of visual aids, let's look at some basics of creating effective visual aids.

Creating Visual Aids

There are some basic guidelines to follow when you create visual aids to use in your speech. Obviously, this book cannot discuss how to create every possible type of visual aid, but you can apply these simple guidelines to any visual you choose to create.

Size: The first and foremost consideration is the size of the visual aid. Nothing

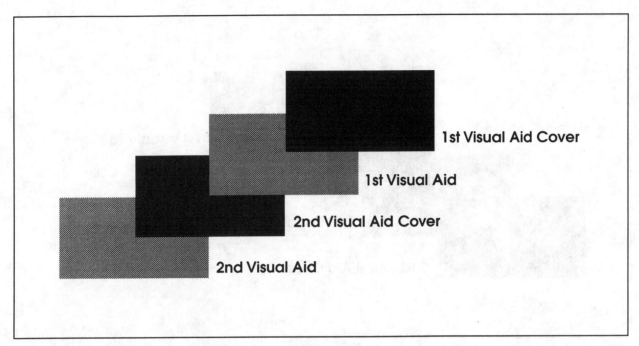

Figure 15. *Each visual aid should have a cover sheet.*

aggravates an audience more than not being able to see what the speaker is talking about. Some speakers believe that if the first few rows can see the visual aid, then use it. **Don't do this!** Every audience member must be able to easily see the visual aid. If they cannot, you're inviting them to stop listening to you. Find out how many people will attend your speech before you create any visual aids. If you use lettering on your visual, keep in mind that half-inch lettering can be seen from up to 10 feet away, and 1 inch lettering can be seen from about 30 feet away.

Lettering Style: If you are using lettering, you should use some type of large block print. Cursive, italic, and unusual font styles are difficult to read from a distance. Make sure your lettering style does not distract the audience.

Color: Visual aids can be created using almost any colors, but try to always contrast dark and light colors. Dark colors on a dark background or light colors on a light background tend to blend together and distort the visual. A light background with dark lettering or illustrations is usually the easiest to see. Also, be aware that red is a power color. If you are giving a speech about the reason why there has been a rise in the sales of your company, use red to show the rising graph line. If you are talking about statistics, use red to illustrate the most important or urgent information.

As you prepare to create the visual aids you want to use, you should first sketch out the visual aids, then look for ways to improve or simplify what you want. Any kind of posters, graphs, charts, or pictures should have at least a two-inch margin on all

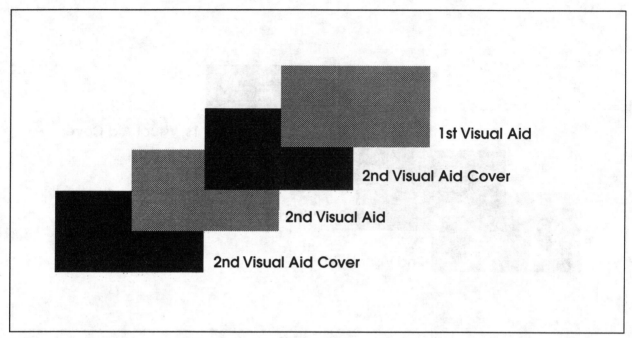

Figure 16. *To present your first visual aid, rotate the front cover sheet to the back*

sides of the visual. Keep the most important part of the visual in the center or very close to it — the audience's eyes will naturally focus on the center.

Methods of Presentation

As you consider using visual aids, you must consider how you will present the visual aids to the audience. Now that we have considered the types of visual aids and the basics of creating visual aids, let's look at presenting visuals to an audience. There are four major methods of presentation. Let's examine each type, how to use it, and its strengths and weaknesses.

Tripod Presentations: Perhaps the most commonly used method of presenting visual aids is a tripod, or "speaker's stand." Most tripods have holding tabs that will sup-

port poster board size sheets up to approximately 30" x 25". Although tripods will hold larger sheets, they are very difficult to manage and are not well supported by the stand. But as a general rule, tripods are effective and a good way to display any graphs, charts, pictures, etc.

There are a few basic rules to remember when using a tripod. First, each visual aid must have a cover sheet (Figure 15). Cover sheets should completely cover the visual aid and be black, dark blue, or some other very dark color. You never want to use a color like red or yellow for a cover sheet because the color will overpower you and cause the audience's attention to repeatedly turn to the visual aid cover. Let's say that you use a red cover sheet. Your clothes would have to be brighter than red in order to keep the audience's attention on you. Dark colors do not distract the audience's

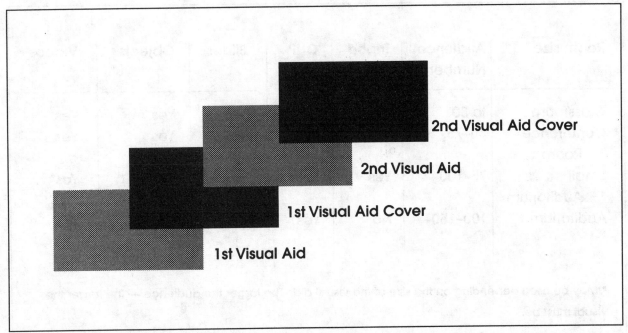

2nd Visual Aid Cover

2nd Visual Aid

1st Visual Aid Cover

1st Visual Aid

Figure 17. *When you are finished with a visual aid, rotate it to the back of the stack and your next cover sheet will be in place*

attention, so make sure you use a dark color.

Next, the visual aids should be arranged on the tripod in order with a cover sheet before each one.

When you come to the section of your speech where you want to present your first visual aid, simply rotate the front cover sheet to the back of the stack as shown in Figure 16.

Once the visual aid is shown to the audience, talk only about what is on the visual aid. You might want to point out certain aspects of the visual aid to the audience, especially if you are using a graph, chart, or map. Once you are finished using the visual aid, simply rotate it to the back and your next cover sheet will be in place (Figure 17). Never leave a visual aid open for the audience to view once you move on to the next

subject because the audience will continue to look at the visual aid instead of listening to what you are saying.

Overall, tripods are easy to use, they do not break down as other types of equipment might, and they are easy to transport. There is one major problem with tripods, however. Air-conditioning vents may blow on your visual aids, causing them to fall off. So, you have to be careful about where you set them up, and you have to be careful not to knock them off yourself as you present your speech!

Overhead Projectors: As with a tripod, an overhead projector (OHP) is a common method of presenting visual aids. Once a bulky machine, many OHPs are now smaller than an average briefcase and are easily adaptable to most speaking situations. OHPs can display a number of types of visual aids

Room size	Audience Number	Tripod	OHP	Slides	Objects	Videos
Classroom	to 30	Yes	Yes	Yes	Yes	Yes
Conference Room	30–75	Yes	Yes	Yes	Yes	Yes
Small Auditorium	75–100	Yes*	Yes	Yes*	Yes*	Yes*
Auditorium	100–150+	No	Yes*	Yes*	No	Yes*

* May be used depending on the size of the visual aid. The larger the audience — the larger the visual must be.

Figure 18. *Major types of presentation methods for certain audience sizes.*

such as charts, graphs, and even pictures. Also, the size of the projection can be easily changed to adapt to even very large audiences, plus OHPs make eye contact very easy since the speaker can glance at the actual transparency instead of having to turn around to see the screen. The only negative aspect of an OHP is you run the risk of the lamp bulb burning out during the speech, so always have a spare bulb just in case.

Now let's look at some basic guidelines for using OHPs.

1. *First, always try to use a screen for the projection.* Even though OHPs will project onto most walls, the appearance of your visual aid will not be as professional. Screens are specifically created to provide high resolution, which a wall cannot provide. If you plan to use an OHP, ask the person who is in charge of the speaking event about providing a screen, or you can even rent one and bring your own.

2. *Do not overcrowd transparencies with information.* Only put the information that you plan to discuss on the transparency.

3. *If you plan to use more than two transparencies, number them to make sure you do not get them out of order.* (This happens frequently and it makes the speaker look unprepared.)

4. *Make sure your transparencies look professional.* Most personal computers will generate quality transparencies and most laser printers will even print them. Additionally, if you have access to a computer, a number of applications are available that will create quality media, such as transparencies, for public speakers. The Resources section at the

end of this book contains several recommendations. You might consider investing in one of these applications.

5. *If you use lettering, make sure you use some type of block print that is easy to read* (as we discussed in the last section). Avoid cursive or other computer fonts that are difficult to read from a distance.

6. *As with all other types of visual aids, don't over do it.*

7. *Make sure you turn off the projector when you are not using a transparency — a blank screen is very distracting for your audience.*

Slide Presentations: A slide presentation can present the same information as an OHP, with a heavy emphasis on photographs of course. Slide presentations are particularly useful for speeches about a trip you have taken or a speech about a certain geographical location or culture.

But slide presentations present a number of potentially serious problems for the speaker, and I personally do not recommend slides for the beginning speaker. Although a slide presentation may present the same information as an OHP, you must give up much of your control to a machine, and you are at the mercy of the machine.

As with an OHP, the bulb may go out during the speech, but more importantly, the machine could jam and slides can easily become out of order or turned the wrong way, which is unlikely with an OHP. Additionally, the room lighting must be much lower for a slide projector, thus making your speech more difficult to perform.

If you decide to use a slide projector, follow the same guidelines for using an OHP, but make sure you have a back-up plan. Should the projector fail, you must know exactly how you will continue your speech without the visual aid.

VCR/Computer Presentations: Technology has greatly enhanced many public speaking occasions during the past several years through the use of video and computers. VCRs now make it possible to show film clips without a film projector, and video projectors can even show videos on screens to almost any size you desire with only a minimal reduction in the room lighting. Personal computers can easily create impressive graphics and visual aids that can be projected by VCRs or OHPs with an overhead projection panel — with only the touch of a button. If you have these resources available to you, you might consider using them for your visual aid presentation, but remember two important points. Once again, make sure that your use of technology directly supports your speech — do not let the technology become your speech. Also, the more equipment you use, the more likely you are to have technical problems during your presentation, so plan carefully.

Now that we have considered the types of visual aids, how to create them, and the methods for presenting them to your audience, you may wonder which type is best for your audience. Of course, you will ultimately have to decide which is best, but the table in Figure 18 may give you some guidance. This table presents the major types of presentation methods for certain audience sizes.

As we complete this chapter, you should decide what visual aid, if any, and what presentation format are best for your speech. If you have decided to use visual aids, you may be wondering what to do if you have equipment problems during the speech. Don't worry! Chapter Fourteen will address this issue. As you plan your visual aids, keep the following check list in mind. You should be able to answer "yes" to these questions. If you cannot, think carefully before using the visual aid.

- **Does the visual aid directly support my speech topic?**

- **Does the visual aid truely help the audience understand what I am talking about?**

- **Is my visual aid easy to understand and not overcrowded?**

- **Will everyone in my audience be able to easily and clearly see my visual aid?**

- **Is my presentation arranged so that the threat of technical failure is minimal?**

- **Do I feel confident using this visual aid and the presentation method I have selected?**

- **Does my visual aid look professional?**

CHAPTER EIGHT

The Verbal Delivery

Now that you have your completed speech and you have made a decision about using visual aids, we will begin working on a number of delivery skills. This chapter focuses on verbal delivery, Chapter Nine focuses on your nonverbal delivery, and Chapter Ten puts all of these skills together and shows you how to practice for your speech.

During these chapters, we will work on many delivery skills and exercises to develop your ability to deliver your speech, but you should understand that a speech delivery is a conglomerate of skills that work together to create an effective presentation.

For our purposes, we will take an effective delivery apart during the next three chapters and look at all of the pieces, but as you begin learning these delivery skills, continue to use them as you work through the rest of the book. For example, after you learn some vocal skills in this chapter, continue using these skills even when you are working on the eye contact section in the next chapter. Delivery skills work together, so practice them together.

I have found that many of my speech students begin to lose their confidence after they have written their speeches and begin to practice, even though they have written effective speeches. I have heard many of my students say, "I'm just not any good at this." Wrong! You already communicate with people everyday — you are simply preparing to communicate in a different way than you do on a day-to-day basis.

Many people think of public speaking as an "art." I prefer to think of it as a "skill." Sure, there are people who are naturally good at public speaking, but good public speakers know what skills are effective and necessary, and they know how to use those skills.

For example, many people know how to build a table, but some people know how to build a table that is attractive, unique, yet functional. The people in the second group were not born with the ability, but they have learned certain skills in table building. The same is true for speakers. They are not born — they are developed! An Olympic athlete has natural ability, but it takes a lot of skill, work, and practice to win a gold medal. So be confident — you can be an effective speaker! After all, that's the purpose of this book. So let's start building your skills.

As we learned in Chapter One, the purpose of your speech is to communicate a message to a group of people. The age of **perfect speeches,** where the speaker was more interested in how he sounded than what he actually said, has gone out of vogue in our information and communication society. The information you share is much more important than your performance, yet it is through your delivery that your message will be understood and received, and one of your major delivery tools is, of course, your voice.

The purpose of this chapter is to develop and strengthen the voice you have — the purpose is not to make you sound like someone else, and this should not be your goal. You may have heard a speaker who had an effective vocal delivery and thought, "I wish I sounded like that." **Do not try to copy someone else's voice.** It's impossible, and you will sound like you are trying to copy someone else — so be yourself.

As we get started, let's understand the basic mechanics of your voice and how sound is produced. Our ability to speak is a fascinating and complex process that we seldom give thought to during our day-to-day routines. When we speak, air is forced from the lungs through the trachea and larynx by the diaphragm and the abdominal and chest muscles. The muscles in the opening of the larynx, called **vocal chords,** move close enough together to vibrate the air as it passes through them. This process is called **phonation.** This sound is **resonated,** or

made stronger, as it passes through the mouth and nasal cavity. The sound is then changed by **articulators,** which are the tongue, lips, palate, and teeth. It is through these articulators that you create words and create the pronunciation for those words.

Now let's make this confusing. We often think of verbal communication as simply speaking, yet there is a nonverbal element I want to introduce. This nonverbal element is often called **paralanguage,** or something that helps language. Paralanguage includes the emphasis you give words, the loudness of your voice, the "feelings" of certain words, and other sounds you produce such as laughing or crying. It is through paralanguage that we give words certain meanings in a context. We will refer to this idea in the next several sections.

Vocal Characteristics

In order to improve your vocal delivery, there are four major voice characteristics you should understand and work to improve. Let's consider these four characteristics. I'll provide you with some exercises later in the chapter to strengthen each of these.

Pitch: Your voice is a lot like a musical scale, and pitch refers to the highness or lowness of your voice. This is one way we all use paralanguage. Your vocal pitch is created by the tightness of your vocal chords. Although all of us can easily speak at a number of pitches, we tend to naturally speak in one major area. As a general rule, the pitch of your voice is not something to be concerned with, unless you have an unusually high voice. If you do, you can lower your pitch some by simply concentrating on lowering it when you speak. The exercises provided later in the chapter will give you the opportunity to practice lowering your voice if your pitch is extremely high.

Volume: Volume is the loudness of your voice. Your volume is created by forcing air through the vocal chords with your abdominal muscles. You can test this by simply placing your hands on your sides with your fingers on your stomach. Say your name in a normal speaking tone, then say your name as loudly as you can without screaming. You will be able to feel your stomach muscles contracting as you forcefully move air through your vocal chords. Obviously, during a speaking situation, your volume is extremely important since all audience members must be able to hear you.

Rate: Rate is the speed at which you speak, and this speed varies greatly from person to person. As a general rule, most of us speak between 130 and 190 words per minute. But speaking rate can greatly damage a speech's effectiveness. I'm sure you have listened to someone who talked so slowly that you wanted to finish his or her sentences, and you have listened to someone who talked so quickly that you could not keep up. In a speaking situation, you want to find the happy median between these two. You want your audience to be able to understand you, but you do not want to drag out your sentences either.

Quality: Quality is the sound of your voice — or the tone. The quality of your voice is primarily created by your articulators — the tongue, palate, teeth, and lips. This affects how you say your words, your

pronunciations, and it affects the overall sound of your voice. Sometimes people have a "breathy" or "nasal" voice, and this is created by resonation. Overall, you want to strive for a balanced, pleasing voice, and the exercises will help you develop quality.

Common Vocal Problems

Obviously, these four characteristics do not exist on their own, but they all work together to create an effective speaking voice. As we have already learned, when you speak to an audience, you want to use a conversational tone. We worked on this when we completed your final draft, but you have to be able to deliver your speech to the audience so that it sounds conversational. When we talk to each other, we use a variety of pitches, volumes, rates, and qualities — depending on what we are talking about. This quality is called "vocal variety."

Consider, for example, how you speak when you tell someone about a boring workday you have had as opposed to a near traffic accident. Your vocal variety changes, depending on the subject and the emotions tied to that subject. Yet, when people present speeches, three common vocal problems can occur. These problems tend to occur because of stress and a focus on the presentation instead of the content. Let's consider these three problems.

First, some speakers use a **monotone voice.** We are all familiar with this, and more than likely, you have had the unfortunate experience of listening to a speaker who used a monotone voice. A monotone voice occurs when a speaker uses the same pitch, volume, and rate for every word, sentence, or paragraph of the speech. Of course, a conversational tone is impossible with a monotone voice because the speaker sounds like a computer spouting out information rather than someone actually talking with the audience. We should note that some people tend to naturally speak in a more monotone voice than others, but we will work on some exercises to avoid this problem.

A second common problem is **repeating vocal pattern.** This is even more frequent in public speaking situations. Repeating vocal pattern occurs when every sentence sounds the same because of rate and pitch. The sentence will either begin or end on the same pitch with the same rate. This produces a singsong effect. Repeating vocal pattern happens when the speaker worries more about the actual sentences he or she is saying than actually talking with the audience. We will also work on this problem.

The final problem that plagues many public speakers is the use of **filler words.** Filler words are simply words or sounds that fill time as the speaker is thinking or preparing to move onto a new idea. Some common examples are "ummm," "O.K.," "all right," "like," "you know," and the ever famous "aaaaaa."

Many speakers are shocked to watch a video of their performance and discover that they constantly use a particular filler word or sound. I once worked with a student who constantly said "O.K." during his speech. When I would tell him to avoid this filler, he would adamantly say that he had not said "O.K." during his speech. He was completely surprised when he saw his video. So be very careful about using filler words and sounds. They can appear without you even realizing it, and they are very irritating to an audience.

Effective Vocal Delivery

Fortunately for us all, there is no perfect "public speaker voice." Each person's voice is just as unique as his or her appearance, and a wide range of vocal styles can be effective in public speaking. Yet, there are some basics of effective vocal delivery that successful speakers use. Let's examine a practical list of "do's and do not's" of vocal delivery, then we'll work on some exercises.

1. *Do talk with your audience.* This is the basis of what we have worked on during the last several chapters. Think about your content and prepare to talk with your audience about your ideas. A speaker who believes in his or her speech will vocally deliver that feeling to his or her audience.

2. *Do talk loud enough.* Never depend on microphone equipment to make your vocal delivery effective. If you will be using a mike, practice and prepare your speech as if you are not — this will develop your vocal strength.

3. *Do use expression in your voice.* Remember that you are trying to communicate meaning to your audience. Believe in what you are saying!

4. *Do pronounce your words carefully.* We will spend an entire section working on this in a few minutes.

5. *Do not speak too quickly.* This is a common problem public speakers experience because stress and excitement generally cause people to talk at an increased rate. Be prepared to monitor your speaking rate when you perform.

6. *Do not use filler words such as "ummmm" and "O.K."* You may not notice this, but your audience certainly will!

Verbal Delivery Exercises

Now we are ready to begin working on some exercises. Remember that the purpose of these exercises is to build verbal communication strength — not to make you sound like someone else. The exercises are divided into sections which focus on certain problems, but try to incorporate all of the skills you have learned as you work on each section.

Articulation: Articulation refers to the actual sound and pronunciation of the words you use. A general rule is to speak clearly and carefully pronounce every sound in each word. Before we try some exercises in articulation, let's look at a list of troublesome words that are commonly mispronounced.

- *Often.* The correct pronunciation is "ofen." There is no "t" sound in "often."
- *The.* For some reason, speakers sometimes begin pronouncing this word as "thee" instead of "thuh," which is natural in common speech. "Thuh" is natural and "thee" makes you sound like you are trying to recite a Shakespearean play.
- *Congratulations.* This word is pronounced "Con - grat - you - lations" yet we sometimes pronounce it "Con - grad u - lations."
- *Get.* This is commonly pronounced "git." The correct pronunciation is "g - et."
- *Picture.* The correct pronunciation is "pic - ture" - not "pic - sure" or "pitcher."
- *Just.* This is sometimes pronounced "jist." The correct pronunciation is "j - ust."
- *February.* The correct pronunciation is "Feb - ru - ary," not "Feb - u -ary."
- *Government.* The correct pronunciation is "govern - ment," not "gover -ment."
- *Library.* "Li - berry" is commonly used instead of "li - brary."
- *Probably.* "Prob - ly" is sometimes used instead of "pro - bab - ly."
- *Family.* A sound is sometimes left out. The correct pronunciation is "fam - i - ly," not "fam - ly."
- *Ask or Asked.* This is sometimes pronounced with an "x" instead of a "k" so the word sounds like "ax" or "axed."

Obviously, these are not the only problem words, but these words are some of the most frequently mispronounced. Go back to the list and say each word correctly several times, listening carefully to the correct pronunciation.

Now let's work on a paragraph that contains most of these words. Say this paragraph out loud several times, focusing on your articulation. You may consider tape recording or video recording yourself to check your progress, or have someone listen to you and offer suggestions.

One of the greatest joys in life is the birth of a child. This new addition to one's family is often a great turning point. After all of the congratulations on the new baby — and the hundreds of pictures — the work truly begins. Child rearing is probably one of the most important jobs on earth. Most libraries contain many volumes of instruction on raising children, and even the government promotes many important programs. Just remember to get the best advice possible and ask questions frequently.

After you practice this paragraph, read your speech text out loud and notice your articulation. Are there words you are mispronouncing or failing to enunciate? Remember that you do not want to sound like a computer, but you should note any words or phrases that seem to give you problems.

Finally, work on your articulation during your daily routine. Practice carefully pronouncing your words. Avoid slurring your words together or dropping the "ings" or "eds" on the end of words. You might want to ask a family member or close friend to point out your vocal weaknesses so you can work on these.

Volume: Now let's work on an exercise to increase the strength and volume of your voice. Obviously, there is one very simple rule that many speakers seem to forget. You cannot speak to an audience using the same volume you would use to speak to a few friends. You may say, "But I will have a microphone, so I don't have to worry about volume." **A microphone is not a replacement for vocal volume.** It is extremely important that you accept this idea.

Later in this book, we will spend an entire section discussing the use of microphones, but you should never depend on a machine to make your delivery effective. Remember that a microphone only projects the voice that you create. Most mike systems that public speakers use do not enhance the voice, and volume adds to the richness and fullness of the voice. So let's work on volume.

As we already discussed, volume is created by the air you force through your vocal chords. So the louder you speak, the more air you will require. As a general rule, you want to strive for a solid, pleasing volume that can easily be heard by every member of your audience. Of course, you do not want to yell at your audience members, but they must be able to hear you. Read the following paragraph as if you are talking to a friend sitting in your living room. Remember to include the articulation skills you have already developed.

If you decide to purchase an automobile, there are many important ideas to consider. The first and foremost consideration is, of course, the cost of the car. Most car payments begin at $200 per month and rise quickly from that point. You must also consider the insurance coverage for the type of car you are interested in buying. Although most of us want more than we can reasonably afford, your budget should be your first concern.

Now that you have read this paragraph out loud several times, let's work on your volume. Stand and say this paragraph in your living room, but this time, pretend that someone in your kitchen must be able to easily hear you. Say the paragraph several times, noting the extra amount of air needed to project the words.

Once you have done that exercise, consider two more. Stand outside the front door of your house or apartment and pretend that someone standing at your mailbox must be able to hear you. If that distance is unreasonable, pick another object, such as a car, that you can speak to. Obviously, there will be some background noise, but I want you to overpower this noise. If practicing your volume outside is not practical, then try the next exercise.

Turn on your television and set the volume at a normal level for viewing. Now, face away from the television and say the above paragraph out loud several times, projecting your voice at a greater volume than the television. You will find that the noise is distracting and irritating, but this practice is good for you. Of course, you will not have to speak over a television set when you present your speech, but you should be prepared to compensate for any background noise. You never know what obstacle you may face when you give a speech, so be prepared.

Finally, begin practicing increasing your volume during your daily routine. This does not mean that you have to talk too loudly, but get in the habit of filling your lungs with air and projecting your voice when you speak. Remember, volume is simply a skill that you can develop, and that development comes through practice.

Pitch: The pitch of your voice is one of the major components of conversational tone. In other words, pitch is one of the ways that we assign meaning to certain ideas. Read the following sentences out loud, noting the intended meaning in parentheses after each sentence.

1. I can't believe this has happened! (shock)
2. I can't believe this has happened. (mild surprise)
3. I can't believe this has happened! (anger)
4. I can't believe this has happened. (sadness)

Did you notice your pitch differences for each sentence? More than likely, your pitch tended to rise or fall, depending on the meaning you intended to communicate. It is through these various pitch levels that words have additional meanings. This is why a monotone speech or a repeating vocal pattern speech is so ineffective. As we already noted, the actual language is only a part of the vocal communication — the meaning assigned to those words is what truly communicates the message — and your pitch helps convey that message. Read the following paragraph about a vacation experience out loud. Pretend that you had a wonderful time on this vacation.

> By noon, we had reached the canyon floor. We spent hours in the canyon looking for old relics. Once we finished, we began the long trail ride home.

Now read the passage as if you had a miserable time on this trip. Notice the difference? Your pitch changes according to your feelings. So how does this affect your speech? Again, your pitch assigns meaning to your words. Of course, you do not want to sound like a bad actor reciting lines, but you want to vary your pitch pattern, depending on what you are talking about.

At this time, you should read your speech noting the pitch changes. Is your use of pitch effective? Does it add to your audience's understanding? Try tape recording yourself and listening to your speech pattern, or ask a friend or family member to listen to you and offer improvement suggestions.

Rate: Although your speaking rate is not something you need to practice, let's take a quick test to make sure your speaking rate is not too fast or too slow. Use a second hand or stopwatch to time yourself reading the following paragraph. Read out loud in your normal speaking voice.

```
    Like other space probes,
such as Viking I and Mariner
10, the Voyager mission
focused on information gather-
ing.  Voyager consisted of a
large satellite dish and a
magnetic boom for measuring
the magnetic field that sur-
rounds planets. Other instru-
ments that could gather infor-
mation, such as wind speeds on
the planet surfaces and atmo-
spheric temperatures, were
also included.
```

Your time for reading this paragraph should be between 17 and 21 seconds. This is a normal speaking rate that audiences will be able to understand. If your time was less than 17 seconds, you are probably speaking too fast — practice slowing down your speaking rate during your daily routine. If your time was over 21 seconds, you are probably speaking too slowly. This may cause your audience to get bored, so practice speeding up your delivery rate.

In summary, remember that an effective delivery combines all of the skills that we have worked on in this chapter. These characteristics create vocal variety and a pleasant vocal quality for your audience. Remember...

- **Carefully pronounce your words.**
- **Do not talk too quickly or too slowly.**
- **Vary your vocal pitch.**
- **Concentrate on what you are talking about — do not concentrate on the sound of your voice.**

Now turn to Chapter Nine to continue our discussion of effective delivery skills. Continue to practice the skills you have learned in this chapter as we work on other skills.

The Nonverbal Delivery

I know what you're thinking. You are probably thinking, "I'm just interested in getting through this speech. I really don't have time to worry about theoretical ideas such as 'nonverbal communication.'" After all, you have your speech written, you have worked on and improved your vocal skills, and now all you need to do is practice, right? Wrong. No matter how good your speech may be, or no matter how strong your voice may be, an effective delivery hinges on your nonverbal communication. It's what separates the effective speaker from the ineffective speaker — and I want you to be an effective speaker.

But is nonverbal communication really that important? Yes. In fact, current communication research has discovered time and time again that nonverbal communication is the most important component of any communication event. Most of our communication, even when we are speaking, is through nonverbal means, so your nonverbal communication is vitally important to the success of your speech.

Human communication is extremely complex. A multitude of books have been written about nonverbal communication, and it remains one of the most interesting fields of study. For our purposes, we are going to look at the basics of nonverbal communication while keeping our focus on public speaking, of course.

So let's begin with a basic definition of nonverbal communication. Simply put, nonverbal communication is any communication, intended or not, that is not language. We often think of nonverbal communication as "silent communication." However, this is not true. We all have the ability to produce sounds, such as laughing, crying, screaming, that are not actually language, and all of these are considered nonverbal communication. So, verbal communication is words, nonverbal communication is everything else.

Before we begin working on your nonverbal delivery skills, you should consider some basic truths about nonverbal communication. These three simple ideas will help you understand some of the material later in this chapter.

1. *Nonverbal communication is cultural.* We learn our nonverbal behaviors from our parents and those around us, and nonverbal behaviors vary from country to country and even within our own nation depending on our cultural group. For example, a hand gesture that communicates one message in one cultural group may have an entirely different meaning in another.

2. *Nonverbal communication is situational.* In other words, the meaning of a nonverbal behavior depends on the situation. For example, the nonverbal behavior of crying means sadness and a feeling of loss at a funeral while this same behavior at a wedding generally communicates joy. It's the same behavior, but the meaning is different depending on the situation.

3. *Nonverbal communication is more powerful than verbal communication.* Consider this situation: A speaker approaches the podium and says, "I am very happy to be here today," but the speaker avoids making eye contact with the audience, does not smile, and seems uncomfortable. The verbal and nonverbal communication contradict each other. The speaker states that he is "happy to be here," but his nonverbal communication says that he is not. So which one will you believe? You will believe the nonverbal communication — every time!

This chapter focuses on two major types of nonverbal communication that will provide you with effective skills for public speaking. First, we will discuss each skill, and then I'll provide you with some exercises.

Body Communication

Body communication, sometimes called **kinesics,** is simply any communication created by your body. This includes eye contact, gestures, expressions, posture, as well as many others. Body communication is the most important type of nonverbal communication for public speakers, and we will spend most of this chapter thinking about and working on body communication

issues. Since body communication includes a wide variety of communication behaviors, let's look at these individually and discuss their importance in public speaking.

Eye Contact: Out of all of the possible nonverbal skills you can possess, eye contact is probably the most important. Yes, I'm sure you know that you are supposed to make eye contact with your audience, but there's much more to it! Let's look at the basics of eye communication.

1. *The eyes communicate cognitive messages.* In other words, the eyes have the ability to replace verbal communication. We all learn this at an early age from our parents. A simple "look" from mom or dad was often enough to change our behavior if we were doing something wrong. The same principle applies to us as adults. If you ask for a day off from work, you can usually anticipate your boss' response by the expression in his or her eyes.

2. *The eyes express emotion.* Think about it. Our eyes have the ability to express every emotion that we can feel — sadness, joy, pain, sorrow, fright — and the list goes on and on. Your eye contact expresses how you feel about an issue. It will tell your audience if you are sincere or not.

3. *The eyes communicate power.* Just as the eyes have the ability to communicate emotions, they have the ability to communicate your competence and ability. If a speaker does not make direct eye contact with the audience, his or her credibility suffers greatly. The audience generally thinks that the speaker is unsure of himself or herself, and thus, unsure of the message.

So how should you use eye contact when you give a speech? There are a few simple techniques that you can learn that

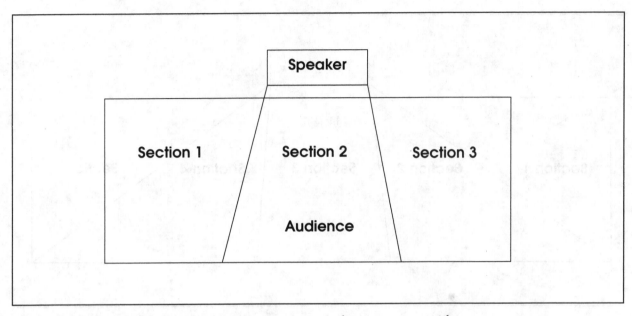

Figure 19. *The speaker has three major sections to make eye contact with.*

will greatly enhance your effectiveness. First, you must make solid, direct eye contact with your audience. You have probably heard or possibly even read that a speaker should simply look over the heads of his or her audience instead of actually looking at them. This does not work! Give your audience some credit — they will know what you are doing, and it makes you look like you are afraid of them. This does not mean that you should try to make direct eye contact with every person in your audience. Depending on the size of your audience, this may not even be possible. Generally, I try to divide my audiences into sections, depending on the size, and try to make eye contact in those sections. You can make direct eye contact with different people in each section throughout the speech without trying to lock eyes with each person. Let's say that you are giving a speech to an audience that is between 25 and 50 people. You will probably need to divide the audience into three major sections. Consider the model shown in Figure 19.

As you can see in this model, the speaker has three major sections that he or she should make eye contact with. This ensures that you do not begin looking at only one section. All too often, public speakers tend to make eye contact in the center, or Section 2 in the model. This tends to close out two-thirds of your audience, and this is not what you want to do. Remember that you want to include your audience in your speech. How can they feel included if you do not look at them? Using sections as in the model will help you avoid leaving out some part of the audience.

But what if your audience is larger? There's one simple rule. The larger your audience, the more sections you need to mentally establish. Let's say that you are delivering a speech to an audience of 400. You might need to section your audience as shown in Figure 20.

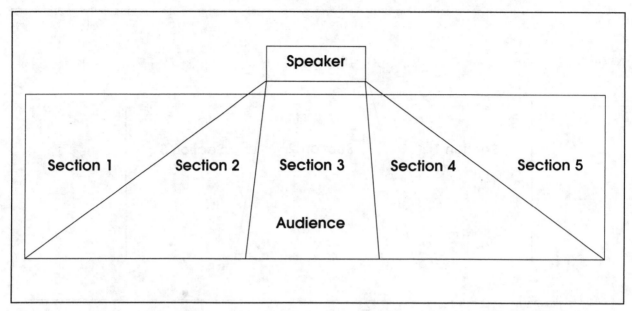

Figure 20. *The larger the audience, the more sections you need to establish for effective eye contact.*

One important point you should realize, however, is that you should not make **sweeping eye contact** with your audience. In other words, do not start at the left of the audience and slowly rotate your head to the right side, then back to the left. Vary the sections in which you make eye contact and do not begin using a certain pattern. This will make your presentation look more natural. Like all speech techniques, effective eye contact takes practice, and I'll provide you with some exercises later in this chapter that will help you.

Facial Expressions: Your facial expressions are vitally important during a speaking situation. Let's consider how facial expressions communicate to people.

1. *Facial expressions communicate cognitive messages and emotions.* Just like the eyes, facial expressions easily replace verbal messages and communicate meaning. For example, facial expressions can communicate happiness, confusion, disbelief, sadness, and a host of other emotions, feelings, and messages.

2. *Facial expressions enhance verbal communication.* If you say that you are excited about an idea, your facial expressions can easily communicate that excitement and enhance the verbal message. Remember that nonverbal communication is more powerful than verbal communication, so if you are talking about your belief in an idea, your facial expressions will have to express your sincerity or your audience may not believe you.

3. *Facial expressions produce "feeling tone."* In other words, the initial "feeling" that an audience has about a speaker comes primarily through facial expression. A speaker's expressions can make an audience feel relaxed with the speaker.

4. *Facial expressions regulate another's communication.* This is a form of feedback.

When someone is talking to us, we "regulate" what they are saying by our expressions. We may act surprised, confused, or even angry, and the facial expressions communicate to the person talking. This is an important point for public speakers. If your audience members look confused, they probably are, and you need to clarify what you are saying. The audience is "regulating" your speech.

During a speaking situation, there are a few simple rules you should follow to use facial expressions effectively.

1. *Be yourself.* Do not try to act like a speaker you have seen. Some people are naturally more expressive than others, so do not try to change your usual expressions.

2. *Do not over do it.* Speakers who are trying to be expressive look like they are trying to be expressive. This will make your face seem animated rather than realistic.

3. *Think about what you are saying.* Do not be so concerned about your facial expressions that you are not paying attention to what you are talking about. Remember that we all use facial expressions every day without consciously thinking about them, so concentrate on what you are talking about, believe in what you are talking about, and your body will do the rest.

4. *Smile before you begin speaking.* A warm smile just before you begin speaking creates positive feelings and helps your audience feel good about you. Surprisingly, a simple smile can even help your performance by making you feel more confident and at ease.

Hand Gestures: Hand gestures are another type of body communication that can greatly enhance a speech, or distract the audience, depending on how they are used.

As with all other nonverbal behaviors, some people tend to use hand gestures more than others. Some of us even use them when we are talking on the phone! Let's consider how hand gestures communicate.

1. *Hand gestures can provide symbols that replace verbal messages.* We all create symbols with our hands such as "O.K.," "peace," or we can express numbers or letters. These symbols vary from culture to culture and tend to change over time. For example, our hand symbol for "O.K." is considered a vulgar gesture in some countries! So, speakers have to be careful with hand gestures and think about the audience.

2. *Hand gestures emphasize words.* We all use hand gestures to emphasize words or phrases. This helps make the intended meaning clear. Usually, hand gestures used to emphasize a certain word or phrase are accompanied by a vocal emphasis as well.

3. *Hand gestures illustrate verbal messages.* We all illustrate our verbal messages by using hand gestures. These illustrations greatly help other people understand the communication. Let's say that you are giving someone directions to your home. If you say, "First drive down Lewis Street and turn right at the intersection...," you will probably illustrate that message by using a hand gesture. You may illustrate turning right or you many even point in the general direction of your home. This is why telephone instructions are often misunderstood. The nonverbal communication is critical for understanding the message.

Let's look at some practical points about what you should and should not do when using handgestures.

1. *We use our hands constantly every day, but for some reason, when we stand in*

front of an audience, the hands become strange, foreign objects that we're not sure how to control. Your hands naturally belong by your side, and when you are not gesturing, that is where they should be. Although this may feel uncomfortable, it looks natural. Do not put your hands behind your back, in your pockets, or hold them in front of you. This makes the audience focus on your hands and not on your message.

We will discuss how to hold notes or a microphone in another chapter, but as a general rule, your hands need to remain at your side unless you are gesturing. If you are using a podium, your hands should still remain at your side when you are not gesturing. Some speakers place their hands on the edges of the podium, but this action is distracting and makes you look like you are having to hold yourself up.

2. *When making hand gestures, bring your hands to about chest level to gesture.* Do not make gestures lower than this because the gesture will bring your audience's attention away from your face.

3. *Keep your hand gestures directly in front of you.* Avoid moving your hands to the extreme sides of your body. This will keep your audience's attention focused on you.

4. *As a general rule, keep your fingers close to each other.* Avoid "clawlike" gestures which will distract your audience.

5. *As with facial expressions, keep your attention focused on your subject.* Believe in what you are saying, and your gestures will naturally follow.

Posture: A person's posture can also communicate information to other people. Although posture is usually not a major non-verbal communication behavior in our day-to-day routines, posture is extremely important for a public speaker. Let's consider how posture communicates.

1. *Posture communicates a person's mood.* If you are sick or unhappy, you tend to slouch and look tired. If you are happy or excited, your posture tends to be very correct.

2. *Posture communicates confidence or lack of confidence.* Just as we can communicate information about our mood by our posture, our confidence level is also communicated by posture.

Both of these ideas have serious implications for public speakers, so let's consider these ideas. First, I want to ask you a question. When does a speech actually begin? If you said it begins when the speaker starts talking, your answer is wrong. If you said it begins when the speaker reaches the podium, your answer is still wrong. A speech begins when you enter the building and audience members are able to see you. This includes the time you are sitting in your chair waiting to give your speech, your walk to the front of the room, and of course, the speech itself. The simple truth every public speaker must realize is that audience members begin making judgments about you before you ever walk to the podium. So how can you use posture to communicate positive feelings to your audience? Let's look at some simple, yet very effective ideas.

1. *Before your speech, always sit up straight and appear calm and collected, even if you do not really feel this way.* More than likely, you will be nervous when you speak, and Chapter Eleven will show you how to control stage fright problems. But just

because you feel nervous does not mean that you have to project that to your audience. Just before you are introduced, do not go into a "coma-like" state and try to psyche yourself up. Your audience is already looking at you, and for all practical purposes, you are already on stage. I am not saying this to scare you, but you should realize that your audience is already forming impressions about you while you are sitting at your seat, and you want those impressions to be good!

2. *When it is time for you to present your speech, walk to the front using correct posture.* Stand up straight and do not look down at the floor as you walk. Many of us have a tendency to look down as we walk, but this makes you appear less confident. So, keep your head up and keep your posture formal.

3. *Once you begin your speech, maintain formal posture.* Keep your feet evenly spaced, but do not lock your knees into place! This causes some people to pass out, so try to keep a formal posture while keeping your legs as relaxed as possible.

4. *Although you want to keep formal posture during your speech, do not be so stiff that you look like a soldier.* Remember that the purpose of formal posture is to communicate confidence and good feelings to your audience, but as with all speaking skills, use common sense so that you do not overdo it.

As I stated earlier, your body communication is a major part of your speech delivery. Although body communication is very important to your delivery, there is one other important type of nonverbal communication for public speakers. Let's take a look at this type.

Distance Communication

Distance communication, sometimes called **proxemics,** is another important type of nonverbal communication for public speakers to understand. Distance communication is a person's use of physical space. How close or how far away we stand from certain people communicates information about our relationships with those people. If you think this type of communication does not apply to speaking — just read on! As with body communication, distance communication is a very technical area of study with many interesting implications, but for our purposes, let's look at the basic types of distance communication.

Personal Space: We all have a personal space about us. This area usually extends up to 4 feet from our bodies and is what we consider our private area. Although we all work in different settings and are surrounded by people, there are usually only a few people who invade our personal spaces. A person's spouse and children, and possibly a parent or a very close friend, may invade his or her personal space each day. But for the most part, we do not like for people to invade our personal spaces — even if those people are friends or co-workers. Our personal space is reserved for those who are intimate with us and no one else.

Although we often allow other people, such as a doctor or possibly a family member, to invade our personal spaces, we are not usually comfortable. Consider this example. Have you ever talked to someone who simply stood too close to you when he or she talked? What did you do? More than likely, you gently backed away, trying to put more space between you and that person. If the

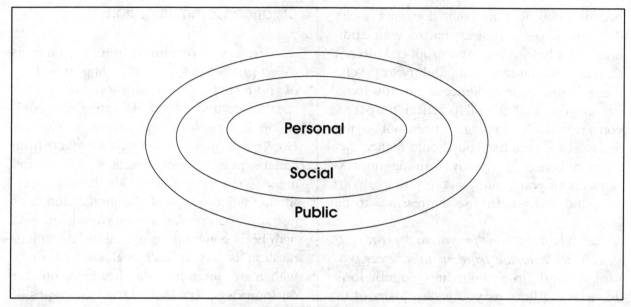

Figure 21. We use personal, social, and public space on a daily basis.

person persisted in being to close to you, you probably became somewhat uncomfortable.

Social Space: Social space is usually 4 to 12 feet and is the space in which most of us function during our day-to-day routine. In social space, we interact with most people that we work with and even our friends and family.

Public Space: Public space is 12 or more feet away and is the space that we tend to keep between ourselves and other people that we are not associated with during our daily routines.

We all use these three types of space (Figure 21) on a daily basis, but how does distance communication affect public speaking? Obviously, the type of space you choose to use communicates to your audience. Let's consider some models, examples, and practical tips to effectively use distance communication in public speaking.

First, simply realize that the three types of distances discussed apply to a public

speaker just as they apply to each person on a daily basis. As we already noted, we all carry "bubbles" of space around us where communication between different individuals takes place. A public speaker must be aware of these spaces and carefully use the space in order to communicate positive feelings to the audience.

So how does a speaker fit into an audience's space and vice versa? Let's add an audience to this model.

Figure 22 presents the basic distance for effective communication. As a general rule, a public speaker should strive to keep his or her audience in social to public space. Depending on the speaking setting, I usually recommend that a speaker stand at least 7 feet from the front row of his or her audience. This is a comfortable distance between you and it. Of course, you do not have to pull out your ruler, but be very careful not to stand too close to your audience. Why is this so important? Let's look at some exam-

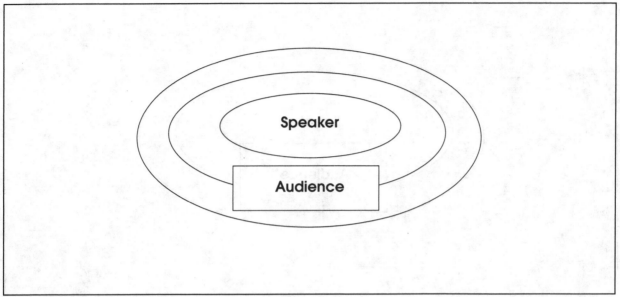

Figure 22. *Basic distance for effective communication.*

ples. Let's move the audience closer to the speaker and discuss the implications.

As you can see in Figure 23, the speaker is now invading the personal space of some of the audience members. Remember that we often become very uncomfortable when someone invades our personal spaces, so in this model, many of the audience members are now uncomfortable. The result? Many of the audience members are now focused on the speaker and not the speaker's message. You never want this to happen. So the simple lesson here is: do not stand too close to the front row — 6 or 7 feet is close enough.

Another idea that relates to this is platform movement. Speakers may move to different areas of the platform, or performance area, in a limited fashion as they present their speeches, but you have probably seen speakers who seem to roam all over the building. At first glance, this may not seem like a bad performance tactic, but let's con-

sider what it does. First, too much movement simply distracts the audience from the message, but again, the movement may invade personal space. The model presented in Figure 24 is of an actual speaker I watched a few years ago. The speaker began speaking at the podium and then moved along the line as shown.

Instead of staying at the platform, this speaker walked up and down the aisles of the audience. His goal, no doubt, was to make himself seem closer to the audience, but the truth is that he invaded the personal space of many of the audience members. Once those members became uncomfortable, they stopped listening to his message. So if you want to use some platform movement, think and plan in advance.

Another aspect of distance communication is presenting your speech too far away from your audience. This tends to have the opposite effect of standing too close to them. Instead of making them uncomfort-

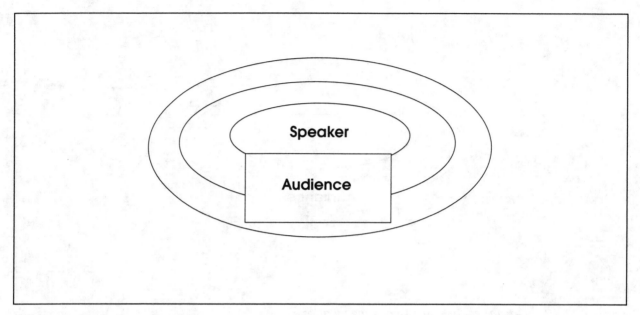

Figure 23. Speaker is invading the personal space of some of the audience members.

able, most audience members will assume that you are uncomfortable and afraid of them. When this occurs, you have put your audience members in public space, they are outside your zone of influence.

Consider this example. Let's say that you are speaking in a room that will seat 100 people. Between the first row and the front wall, there is 12 feet of space. If you take your position close to the front wall, you may appear uncomfortable, uncertain, or even unfriendly to your audience, so try to keep the first few rows of your audience in social space.

You may wonder how practical this information is since most speaking settings are arranged by someone else before the event. Let me tell you a secret — most people who arrange the chairs and platform for a speaking event are not public speakers themselves. Often, you can suggest how you want the room arranged, and most people in charge of speaking events will be happy to accommodate you. Chapter Thirteen will discuss this idea further.

In summary, simply realize that distance communicates information to people and often helps them form initial impressions about you, and you want those impressions to be positive. Remember not to stand too close or too far away from your audience, and simply use common sense.

Nonverbal Delivery Exercises

Now that we have discussed the two major forms of nonverbal communication that affect public speaking, let's spend some time practicing some exercises to develop your nonverbal communication skills. Although the exercises are divided into sections that work different skills, remember to continue to practice your verbal communication skills as you work on these sections.

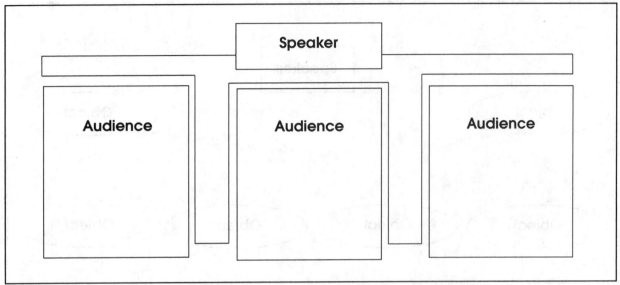

Figure 24. Instead of staying at the platform, this speaker walked up and down the aisles of the audience — invading the personal space of many audience members.

Eye Contact: For these exercises, you will need to get six objects that you can easily move around the room, such as six plastic cups or six small candles. These objects will serve as markers for some exercises in eye contact.

Select a longer section of your speech in which you are most familiar and take the six objects to the largest room in your home or office. Select a place to say your speech, then place the objects as shown in Figure 25.

Now, say the section you have selected while making eye contact with the three of the objects. Remember...

- Do not rotate your head from side to side — vary your pattern.
- Do not begin using a repeating head movement. In other words, do not look at object two, then object three, then object one and begin repeating the same movements.

- Pretend the objects are the eyes of your audience members — look directly at them, not over them.

Practice this two or three times then move on to the next exercise. Now, concentrate on making eye contact with four of the objects.

Sometimes audience members may be sitting to the extreme right and left of the speaker, depending on the room arrangement. That is why you should learn to make eye contact with all six objects. Repeat the section at least three times; remember not to begin using a pattern.

Hand Gestures / Facial Expressions:
As we already noted, each person tends to use hand gestures and facial expressions differently. Some people naturally use more hand gestures and facial expressions than others, but we all "talk with our hands and faces" to some extent, and you want to use your hands and make facial expressions

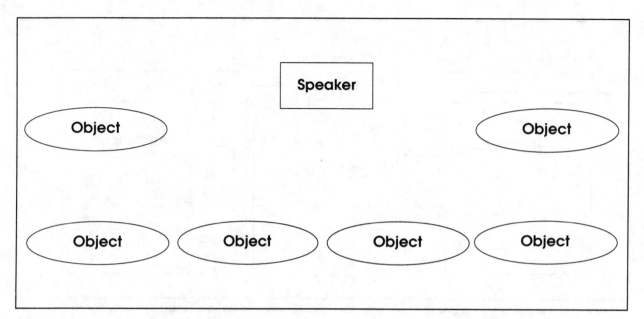

Figure 25. *Practice making eye contact without moving your head or falling into a pattern.*

when you speak. The following exercises primarily help you practice what not to do.

First, use the same section of your speech that you used for the eye contact exercises. Stand in front of a standard size table, such as a kitchen table, and place your speech in front of you on the table. Select three or four objects near you to be your focal points for eye contact. Now, say the section of your speech, keeping your hands at your sides without making any gestures. Remember to practice your eye contact and continue to practice your vocal skills such as enunciation and volume. Repeat this three times so that you will get used to the feeling of keeping your hands at your sides. Remember...

- Keep a formal posture, but do not look like a soldier.
- Let your hands relax at your side — do not place your palms flat against your legs.

Now, practice the same section several times again, this time making hand gestures and facial expressions. You may want to use a mirror so you can watch yourself. Remember these important ideas:

- Concentrate on what you are saying. Your hands and face will naturally follow you when you concentrate on your message.
- Do not use both hands every time you gesture. This tends to make you look awkward and your gestures will become very repetitive.
- Make your gestures at chest level — do not gesture lower than this because the gestures will distract the audience's attention from your face.
- When you make a gesture, let your hands return to your side. Do not hold them together at your waist, put them in your pockets, or behind your back. You may find this exercise awkward at first, but continue to practice.

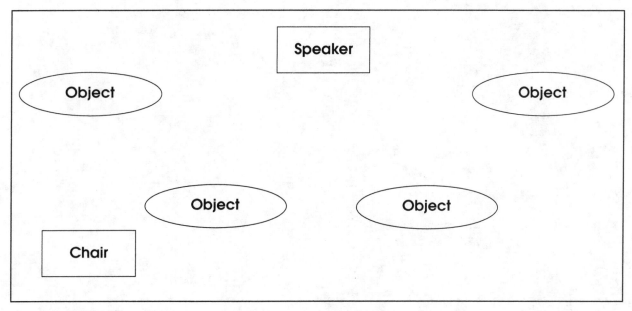

Figure 26. *Practice walking to the platform while maintaining proper posture. Do not look at the floor.*

Posture: Finally, let's add the last major component of body communication - your posture. Once again, you will use the same section of your speech as you did in the previous exercise, four or five of the objects for eye contact, and you will need a chair. Use the largest available room in your home, or wherever you may be practicing for your speech, and arrange the room as shown in Figure 26.

Select a position for the speaker's platform, arrange the objects, and put the chair behind the objects facing the platform.

Now, sit in the chair and notice your posture. Sit up straight and keep your head up. Imagine that someone is at the platform introducing you. Now, stand and walk to the platform. Maintain formal posture and do not look at the floor as you walk. When you reach the platform, smile - then begin the section of your speech, using all of the skills you have learned so far. Keep your feet close together and stand evenly on each leg. Practice this at least three times, beginning at the chair.

As we complete this chapter on nonverbal delivery, keep the following major ideas in mind at all times.

- **Always let your nonverbal behaviors be message driven. Everything you do should strengthen your message.**
- **Concentrate on what you are saying, and your nonverbal communication will enhance your message.**
- **Do not try to become someone you are not. Work to strengthen your own nonverbal delivery skills and do not try to act like someone else.**

Now that we have thought about your verbal and nonverbal delivery skills and worked on some exercises, we are ready to finally put all of this information together and practice your speech. You are very close to becoming an effective public speaker!

CHAPTER TEN

Practice!

Great speakers, no matter how diverse, always have one thing in common — they know that the key to success is practice. People are not born with the ability to deliver effective speeches. The many skills we have discussed take time and practice to develop. But even people who have given hundreds of speeches realize that practice is the key to a good presentation. There is a common myth that great speeches tend to fall into place once you are behind the podium, but this never happens. This chapter shows you how to move your speech text to a presentation format, how to practice, and how to integrate all of the skills we discussed in Chapters Eight and Nine.

First, let's discuss a common question speakers often ask — should I use a manuscript, or notes, or nothing when I give my speech? Most public speakers have a certain way they present the text of their speeches. Also, most public speakers or speech teachers are adamant about which type is best. Let's discuss each type, its strengths and weaknesses, and come to a decision about which type is best for you.

First, many speakers use a **manuscript.** This simply means that the entire speech is written in an essay type form, placed in a binder, and used as the speaker presents the speech. The president, most members of Congress, and most other televised speakers use a manuscript. Some live speakers also use a manuscript, but this is not as common.

There are some advantages. First, the complete speech is in front of you, so you avoid getting confused or saying phrases that are unclear or can be misconstrued by audience members. The problem, however, is presenting the speech in a manner so that you do not sound like you are reading to the audience. Making eye contact is also difficult since you may easily lose your place in the text. Most televised speakers have the luxury of using a teleprompter, a machine that scrolls the text in front of the speaker at eye level so he or she never has to look down at any printed text. But for our purposes, a manuscript speech is probably not your best option. It may sound like the safest and easiest, but using a manuscript to present a speech requires great skill.

Notes are the most commonly used presentation aid. Notes are simply your basic text placed on note cards. The note card method is generally very effective since it keeps your information organized, allows for eye contact, and avoids the reading problem. However, note cards can easily get out of order, and you stand the chance of forgetting examples and ideas you intended to present.

Finally, the **memory method** is good and is impressive to your audience, and this is the method I normally use. First, when a speaker approaches the platform and begins speaking without the aid of notes or a manuscript, he or she is automatically held in high esteem by the audience since this method makes you appear totally prepared and knowledgeable.

However, there are some major problems. First, you stand a great chance of getting confused and blanking out. This is a common problem and has affected almost every speaker at one time or another. I remember listening to a speaker once who was using the memory method. He was a good speaker and well prepared, but during his speech he suddenly fell silent. He began to stumble and ad lib as he tried to get back on track in the text of his speech. He never recovered. Although he made it through the presentation with the help of a sympathetic audience, his speech was basically a disaster. We do not want this to happen to you!

Although I usually do not use any notes when I speak, I do not recommend this method to people who do not have experience. As we have seen over and over again, we all have different skills. Some people are simply good at speaking this way while others would never do a good job with a memorized text — and this is not the time to find out if you have natural skills with memorization.

So, which type is best for you? I rec-

ommend that you use a combination of notes and memorization. This way, you are able to work on memorization, but you are not left alone at the podium without some backup.

Let's talk about **memorization** for a few minutes. Memorization generally does not mean that you memorize your speech word for word, although some speakers do choose to do this. Unless you are an experienced speaker, you are asking for trouble if you take this approach, and even experienced speakers still find themselves in "hot water" occasionally. The way to memorize a speech is not to memorize the words, but the ideas that you are working with.

Generally, you should memorize your introduction, since the audience's first impression of you and your speech comes during the introduction. You want your introduction to be as flawless as possible. Second, memorize your transition statements between each section. This way, if you begin to have trouble with a section of your speech, you can always move to your next transition, then to your next section. This is like having a safety net to avoid blanking out during a speech. Also, I recommend that you memorize your conclusion so that you always end on solid ground.

You should begin working on these sections at this time. Do not continue to the next part of your speech until the one before it can be easily said. Work on this, and we will begin Part One of the chapter.

Part One: Note Cards

This section will help you move your speech text to note cards. First, let's consider some basic ideas about note cards, then we'll begin developing your cards.

1. Always number your note cards carefully in either the upper or lower corners of each card. You may want to use a different color ink than your text since this will make the card numbers stand out.

2. Double space.

3. Do not overcrowd note cards — use more instead of less.

4. Print and make your words large.

5. Always use white note cards.

6. Do not write on the back of note cards.

7. Only use 3 x 5" or 4 x 6" sized cards.

Of course, these ideas are very simple, but they will have a great impact on your performance. Consider this note card:

```
     This is an example of an
ineffective note card. The
information contained on this
card is too small and too
close together for the speaker
to be able to effectively use
thecard. Always double space
the card and make sure the
information is easy to read.
```

Now try to present a speech using note cards like the one above. The speech would be very difficult to perform. You should always use more instead of less as far as note cards are concerned. Take a look at this card:

```
     Always make your writing
easy to read and skip lines
within the text. This will
make your delivery much
easier. Make sure you num-
ber each card.
                            1
```

You should only use white note cards, you should not write on the back of cards, and you should use smaller sized cards. First, white is a neutral color that will not distract your audience. Even if you are using a podium to present your speech, white cards are still best because your writing will be easier to read. Note cards come in many colors, but the same rules for note cards apply as visual aid covers — if you use yellow note cards, your clothes and face will have to be brighter than the color yellow in order not to distract the audience.

Secondly do not write on the back of note cards. If you are not using a podium, the audience will be able to see the writing on the back of the cards, but more importantly, you will have to turn each card over to use it — and when you are using several cards, the likelihood of the cards becoming disorganized is great. So do not make your presentation more difficult — only write on one side of the note cards.

Finally, I recommend that you use either 3 x 5" or 4 x 6" note cards. Cards any larger than this will tend to distract your audience and are difficult to manage.

Before you begin moving your speech to note cards, let's consider a few ideas and "tricks" that may help you. You should realize your note card collection is not a term paper that you will be handing to someone to grade. No one will see your note cards but you, so basically, do whatever helps you — and there are several things you can do that may help your delivery.

First, one thing that may help you is to **highlight** words or sections that are particularly troublesome. As you practice on your speech, you will discover places where you tend to make word blunders or "stumble." Highlighting those sections with a marker, or some other means, may remind you to be careful or to slow down. Let's look at an example using one of the speeches from the appendix of this book about Mars' volcanos:

```
    The first, Olympus Mons,
has a base of 435 miles and
is about 15 miles at the
peak — that's three times
taller than Mount Everest,
the tallest mountain on
Earth.  We should note that
mountains this tall can not
exist on Earth — they would
collapse under their own
weight because of our grav-
ity.
                          12
```

In this example, the speaker has trouble pronouncing "Olympus Mons," and tends to stumble over the words "would collapse." By highlighting these words, the speaker remembers to "be careful" during those sections. You can highlight words by using a marker, simply changing the text style as shown in the example, or just by underlining the troublesome words or sections — again, do whatever works best for you.

Another trick that can improve your performance is placing **symbols** in the text of the speech. A symbol simply reminds you of something you need to do while presenting your speech. For example, my greatest delivery problem is talking too quickly. I have to constantly remind myself to slow down my speaking rate. If I were delivering this speech using cards, I might do something like this:

```
    The first, Olympus Mons,
has a base of 435 miles and
is about 15 miles at the
peak — * that's three times
taller than Mount Everest,
the tallest mountain on
Earth.  We should note that
mountains this tall can not
exist on Earth — they would
collapse under their own
weight because of our grav-
ity.
                          12
```

The asterisk (*) would remind me to slow down. Note the placement of the asterisk. The statement "that's three times taller than Mount Everest" is a qualifying example, which we discussed in Chapter Five. The statement helps the audience realize just how gigantic Olympus Mons actually is. So, I would need to slow down as I made that statement so the audience would have time to process the information.

Symbols can be almost anything you want to use, and you can use a combination of symbols to remind you of different problems. You should, however, keep the use of symbols to a minimum so they do not confuse you, and as a general rule, you should not use words. Consider this example:

```
   The first, Olympus Mons,
has a base of 435 miles and
is about 15 miles at the
peak — (slow down!) that's
three times taller than
Mount Everest, the tallest
mountain on Earth. We
should note that mountains
this tall cannot exist on
Earth — they would collapse
under their own weight
because of our gravity.
                         12
```

In this example, the star has been replaced with the actual words the star represents. The problem with using words is that you might actually say the words to the audience, and you would not want to shout "slow down!" in the middle of your speech.

On occasion, using words that give you instructions may be useful, if you are very careful. I had a public speaker friend in college who would never smile during his speeches. No matter what he was talking about, he always looked like he was reciting an obituary for a funeral. After numerous criticisms from his professors and classmates, he started writing "smile!" in large block letters at the top of every note card — and this cured his problem. After giving several speeches, he didn't even need to put this reminder on his cards; it became a natural part of his performance. Again, do whatever helps you, just be careful about writing words on your cards that you do not intend to say to the audience.

One final trick that may help you is the use of **markers.** As you practice your speech, you may notice sections that seem to make you stumble over words, particularly when making eye contact. If this happens, you may want to put a marker on that card that will help you find your place in the text. Consider this example:

```
   The first, Olympus Mons,
has a base of 435 miles and
is about 15 miles at the
peak — * that's three times
taller than Mount Everest,
the tallest mountain on
Earth. # We should note
that mountains this tall
can not exist on Earth —
they would collapse under
their own weight because of
our gravity.
                         12
```

If I were having trouble with this card, I would select a symbol and mark the area that caused problems. The pound symbol (#) on the card above would help me find my place in the text. Again, you can use any symbol or even a colored dot to help you find your place.

Another effective use of markers is to "mark" a visual aid presentation. The markers will help you remember to open and close a visual aid at the correct times.

These tricks may help your performance, and you will probably discover tricks of your own that are helpful to you. Before we move on, let's look at a series of sample note cards to reinforce what you have learned in this section. For these cards, the following symbols are used:

Highlight — helps the speaker identify troublesome words or phrases.

* — Slow down the delivery rate.
# — Marker for eye contact.
Δ — Marker to open visual aid.
∂ — Marker to close visual aid.

Sample Note Cards

During the past hundred years or so, there's been a lot of superstitions about Mars, * but through **techno-logical advancements**, we have learned many interest-ing facts about this planet during the past 30 years. Most of our current infor-mation has come from high-powered telescopes,

3

the Voyager missions, which photographed the planet, and the Viking probes,

which landed on Mars and performed soil tests of the

alien landscape. # Let's consider some of the facts this research discovered: — Mars is approximately 142 million miles from the sun and the Martian

4

year lasts 687 days. Mars has two small moons — Phobos and Deimos, both of which look like flying potatoes and are probably asteroids that were caught in Mars' orbit some time in the past. * Mars is only half the size of Earth, and because of Mars' small size, the surface gravity is

5

smaller also. If you weigh 200 pounds on Earth, * you would only weigh about 76 pounds on Mars — sounds like a great diet plan! Δ But low gravity does cause some problems. For one, there isn't much of an atmosphere. Earth's gravi-ty keeps its atmosphere wrapped around it like a coat, but

6

Mars' gravity allows most
of its atmosphere to escape
into outer space. Most of
the air is carbon dioxide —
the gas we all exhale — and
you would need a spacesuit
to survive. If you want to
get a tan, Mars would not
be a good vacation spot.
In the summer, the temperature may rise to a cozy 70
degrees. But on the aver-
age, * the   7

temperature is around zero
and may get as cold as 180
degrees below zero during
the winter — certainly not
swimsuit weather! # But the
planet surface is rather
interesting, and the Viking
missions of the late 70s
gave us the first pictures
of the Martian landscape.
∂ The surface
                              8

of Mars is **actually a reddish-brown color** and is
made up of rocks and desert
terrain. Its surface is
filled with craters, * and
many of the rocks appear to
have come from volcanos.
                              9

At this time, you should select the size of note cards you want to use and move the text of your speech to your note cards. As you begin to practice, you will find trouble-some areas, or places that need a marker or symbol of some kind. You can add those later after you begin practicing. Remember to number your cards and skip lines. Also, since I recommend that you completely memorize your introduction and conclusion, you may want to not include these sections on your cards. Once your speech is written on note cards, move on to the next section.

Speaking with Note Cards

Now that your speech is on note cards, let's take a look at using note cards when you speak. There are a few simple ideas that will make using cards easy and make you an effective speaker. As we have discussed many times before, you may or may not use a podium when you speak. We'll discuss the use of podiums in detail in Chapter Thirteen, but for now, let's consider how to use note cards first with a podium, then secondly without.

If you use a podium, there are a few simple rules to keep in mind. First, try to place the cards toward the front of the podium. Some podiums are tilted so that the cards will slide to the back, and if this is the case, you'll have to put them at the back. But as a general rule, try to place the cards toward the front of the podium as shown in Figure 27.

By placing the cards toward the front of the podium, you will be able to look at the cards with very little head movement. If you have placed the cards toward the back, the cards are closer to you; therefore, you will have to look down to see the cards. This

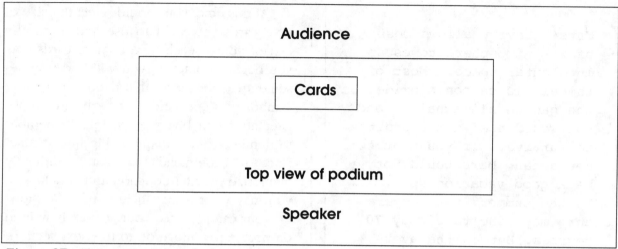

Figure 27. Place note cards to the front of the podium.

begins what I call the yo-yo syndrome. Your head has to move up and down to see the cards and to make eye contact with the audience.

If you do use a podium, then you should *use the podium.* In other words, do not hold the cards in your hands if you are standing behind a podium. This tends to distract the audience.

If you are not using a podium, there are a few performance skills you need to understand and practice. First, hold your note cards with only one hand. You should always use the hand that you write with to rotate the cards — you are less likely to drop a card if you do this. *If you are right-handed, hold the cards with your left hand,* and if you are left-handed, hold the cards with your right hand. When you are ready to move to the next card, simply move your free hand from your side and rotate the used card to the back of the stack. You are free to make gestures with your available hand, but always let your free hand fall to your side when you are not gesturing or rotating a card.

Also, hold the cards at chest level, slightly away from your body. This way, you will be able to see the cards and make eye contact without moving your head. If you hold the cards at waist level, you will have to look down to the cards, and if you hold the cards higher than chest level, the cards will block your face from the audience's view.

Obviously, problems can arise when you use cards, so let's consider a few practical tips to alleviate common note card problems.

1. *A few minutes before you speak, double check your cards and make sure they are in order.* Even if you have already checked them five times, check them once again a few minutes before you will speak. Do not begin shuffling through your cards as you are being introduced. Remember that the audience is already watching you during the introduction.

2. *Once you check your cards for the final time, hold your cards until you walk to the front.* Do not put them in your pocket or a folder of some kind.

3. *If you should drop a card or cards while you speaking, follow these two simple rules.*

- If you drop a card or cards that you will need, pause and pick them up. Let's say that while you are rotating a card to the back of the stack, you drop the last three cards of your speech. Many speakers would try to get through the speech without the use of those three cards, but this is a mistake. Your audience is already distracted since you dropped the cards, so go ahead and correct the problem so they will not be distracted again when you begin stumbling through the final section. There is no need to apologize or give another speech about why you dropped the cards. Simply pick them up and continue your speech.
- If you drop a card or cards that you have already used, do not pick them up. Since you will not need the cards, there is no reason to distract the audience further by picking up the used cards.

Part Two: Practice

Now that we have your note cards completed, you are ready to begin practicing your speech. From this point on, you should only practice with your note cards — do not return to the original written copy of your speech. As you begin to practice, you will discover what works best for you and you will continue to find places in your speech that need minor revisions. Remember to mark sections of your speech that seem to give you trouble as you discover them. Before you begin practicing your speech, let me offer you a few pointers concerning practice.

- You should pretend that you are performing in front of an audience every time you practice your speech. When an Olympic gymnast prepares for competition, he or she practices with the gold medal in mind. You should do the same. Reading over your speech will not help you build your delivery skills. Each time you say your speech, select some objects for eye contact, practice your vocal skills, practice your nonverbal delivery skills, and practice using your cards.
- You may have a concern about remembering all of the many skills we have discussed as you present your speech. One of my students once said, "I can't remember to use my hands, make eye contact, hold my cards correctly, keep my feet evenly spaced, and still get the words right." You may feel this frustration, and that is perfectly normal. But if you practice correctly, you will not have to think about your delivery skills — they will become a natural part of your performance. That's why it is so important that you pretend you are standing in front of an audience each time you practice your speech.
- After you have practiced for a few days, you may want to practice in front of a mirror, or even videotape yourself. I have always found these tools valuable ways to correct minor delivery problems. Another reason for using a mirror or videotape is these tools allow you to "see" all of your delivery skills combined, and this actually helps to teach yourself since you are able to see what you are doing. Of course, we are all different, and some experienced

speakers find using a mirror or watching themselves on video to be very unnerving. If using these tools makes you uncomfortable, then do not use them.

- You should try to practice your speech in a number of different rooms. The best place to practice is the actual room in which you will be performing. If this isn't possible, then try to find a room that is similar in size. A local church, a school, or possibly your place of business may have rooms that are large enough for effective practice.

- Finally, you may want to practice in front of some other people who can give you pointers. The obvious choice is your family, but some people find that practicing in front of family tends to make them more nervous and insecure. You will have to decide this for yourself, but if you choose to practice in front of other people, try to perform for people who will support you, yet offer sound advice.

If you are using visual aids, here are a few practice tips you should consider:

- Work on your speech presentation for several days before you begin practicing with visual aids. If you try to practice your speech and include your visual aids at the same time, you may find yourself very frustrated. Get your speech presentation "roughed in," then add your visual aids.

- Remember to practice eye contact when you use the visual aids — do not get in the habit of looking at the visual aids.

- Of course, you need to practice using visual aids in a number of different rooms, especially a room similar to the one in which you will actually present your speech. This is extremely important if you have decided to use slides or video footage.

Congratulations, you are almost ready to present your speech! Remember that practice is the key to your ultimate success and an effective delivery comes only through practice. You may feeling a little nervous as your "big day" approaches — you may even be scared to death. With that in mind, turn to the next chapter and let's talk about the very important issue of stage fright.

CHAPTER ELEVEN

Taking the Fear Out of Fear

As you have been working on your speech and your delivery skills, you have probably said to yourself, "This is all great — but what happens on the day of the speech when I am scared to death?" If there is safety in numbers, then you are definitely safe. In fact, in a number of national polls, Americans ranked giving a public speech their greatest fear. The second greatest fear was going to the dentist. Death did not even make the top five. This chapter guides you through your stage fright feelings by understanding what creates fear, learning some relaxation techniques, and understanding the common symptoms of stage fright and how to control them.

A public speaker friend once said, "Ninety-five percent of public speakers admit to having stage fright — and the other five percent are liars." Those statistics may not be quite true, but the basic premise is correct. Most people experience some kind of fear before speaking — myself included. Even experienced speakers and public figures have admitted their fear of the podium. Johnny Carson, Merv Griffin, Joan Rivers, and a host of others have spoken about their stage fright problems. You are not alone.

I want us to take a moment to qualify your fear. One of my speech teachers once said to me before a competition, "There's nothing to be afraid of — you are not going to die. No matter what happens, the sun will come up tomorrow." That may be true — but sometimes death may seem like a better option!

Let's face the facts. There are many things to be afraid of when delivering a speech. You are in front of a large group of people, your reputation is on the line, you could make yourself appear incompetent or unprofessional, or you could simply not make any sense. I'm not saying all of this to make you more afraid, but denying a problem does not help solve the problem.

My approach to stage fright may be different from other speakers'. Many people may say, "Just don't think about it and you'll do fine," but when in your life have you ever solved a problem by not thinking about it? Probably never, and stage fright is no exception. The purpose of this chapter is to give you skills that will help you. So, let's admit that stage fright is a problem, let's confront it, and then, let's learn how to control it.

What Is Fear?

First, we need to understand **fear.** Fear is a natural, basic, and much needed component of the mind and body. Fear enables us to escape from danger and avoid problems. It often enables us to make decisions that are in our best interest. Fear primarily comes from our subconscious mind. As you go about your daily routine, your subconscious mind watches your environment closely for problems or feelings you may have about some issue. Sometimes fear can simply give you a bad feeling about something, or it may trigger the fight or flight response. When your subconscious senses a physical threat, it instantly releases adrenaline and other chemicals into the body, pools the blood supply to the major organs, increases the heart and breathing rates, suspends unnecessary functions such as digestion, and completely focuses all brain power on the threat.

Let's look at an example. Let's say that you are out for a leisurely walk in your neighborhood. Your mind drifts from topic to topic, reviews the day's activities, and thinks about problems or future events. Suddenly, a strange dog begins approaching. Your subconscious immediately notices the dog, makes a split second decision, and decides there is danger. Let's say the dog begins barking and running toward you. Instantly, your brain supercharges your body with a number of chemicals, rechannels your blood supply, and speeds up your heart and breathing rates. Your conscious and subconscious focus on the danger and immediately decide to fight or flight. Whatever you do in this situation, your brain has prepared your body for the physical demand of fight or flight.

Now, let's look at a public speaking scenario. You arrive at the building where you will give your speech, and you examine the podium or speaking area; you have practiced, and you are well prepared. As people begin to come into the room, you suddenly feel strange. Your heart speeds up its beating, your breathing rate increases, and your hands and feet turn cold. You begin to notice all of these symptoms, and your brain begins to focus on them. You begin to wonder what is wrong. You're sweating, your heart is pounding, you feel dizzy — and then it dawns on you, "What if I'm having a heart attack!" At this point, the fear can quickly turn into panic.

So what has happened in this scenario? Let's take a look at the body's function. First, you have been working on your speech for some time now. You have spent hours thinking about it, practicing, and hoping you will perform well. Your subconscious senses these anticipatory feelings, nervous thoughts, and general anxiety about the event. Your subconscious stores this information, and on the day of your speech, it connects the speech event with the anxiety you have been feeling. The result — fear. Your body prepares you for fight or flight which surprises you because you know from your conscious mind that there is nothing to fear. Remember our "dog" scenario.

We have all had something like that happen to us, yet we never question the physical symptoms such as a racing heart, dizziness, and shallow breathing because we recognize the immediate threat. In a speech situation there is no physical threat, but your body has prepared you for a physical reaction — fight or flight! Your body has been supercharged for the fight or flight response, yet you do not need a fight or flight response or any other unusual physical energy for the speech since you are not in physical danger. This physical reaction is what causes stage fright.

Confronting Fear

Now that we understand the causes of fear and stage fright symptoms, let's discuss some simple facts. In the next section, you will learn some techniques for controlling fear, but first, I want you to understand some simple truths about public speaking. Read these points over and over during the next several days and believe them.

1. *Fear is a normal reaction.* Very few people deliver speeches who do not experience fear.

2. *Experienced speakers have stage fright problems.* Do not let the appearance of a calm, professional speaker destroy your courage. More than likely, that speaker you see on television is also afraid — he or she has simply learned to control the fear.

3. *Your audience wants to like you.* Often, speakers let their imaginations create images of cruel, mean audiences who hate speakers. This is simply not true. In fact, the opposite is true. Most audience members will give you the benefit of the doubt and forgive you for mistakes. Audience members want to enjoy your speech, they want to learn something, and they want to like you. So let them.

4. *You are in control.* Speakers often have feelings of fear because they feel they are out of control. The opposite is true. In a speaking situation, you are the one who is in control of the room and the audience. The audience gives you this power and they respect it. You could ask your audience members to get out of their chairs and kneel down on the floor for an illustration, and most of them would do it without a second thought. You are in control.

5. *Fear can be useful.* As you learn to control fear, you will probably find it can help your speech by giving you additional energy. Remember that fear supercharges the body, and that energy can be used to your advantage, once you can control it. Speakers who are relaxed and at ease are usually boring. Fear can be used to your advantage.

Taking the Fear Out of Fear!

Now, let's begin to look at some specific tactics for controlling stage fright. First, let's learn three general methods for controlling the symptoms of fear.

1. *Burning Energy:* There is one great rule you should remember at all times. The key to controlling stage fright is to **burn energy.** Remember that fear pours adrenaline and other chemicals into your body and prepares it for a physical reaction. Since you will not need a physical reaction, you need to burn the energy your body has created. Cold, shaking hands; a racing heart; and irregular breathing are all caused by excess energy. So how can you burn it? Ideally, if you could jog around the building before a speech, you would burn a lot of the fear energy and you would calm down. Of course, this isn't possible in a public speaking setting, so you have to resort to some other methods. Let's discuss these:

• *Movement:* Public speakers who sit for thirty minutes before their presentation are usually more nervous than those who do not. Move around the room and visit with people or pace if you can (as long as it is not distracting to others — you don't want to project the image that you are afraid). Depending on the type of meeting, such as a dinner or banquet, you may not be able to move around before your speech. If you can't, use the next method.

• *Muscle Tension/Relaxation Technique:* Another way to effectively burn energy is the **muscle tension/relaxation technique.** You can use this method anywhere and at any time before your speech. Begin with the calves of your legs. Tense these muscles as hard as you can and hold for 10 seconds. Then, relax these muscles. Now move to your thighs and do the same. Continue up your body, tensing and relaxing every major muscle group such as your abdomen, chest, and arms. With a little practice, you can do this without anyone even knowing what you are doing. Again, the idea is to burn energy, and this exercise helps to burn energy in your major muscles and return blood circulation to normal. The trick to this technique is you must practice at home. Do not wait until the day of the speech — you may feel or even look awkward without some practice.

2. *Control Your Breathing:* As you work to burn energy, you must also **control your breathing.** This is the second method of attack. When your body releases adrenaline and other chemicals, it speeds up your heart rate, thus changing your breathing pattern as well. If you go jogging, your breathing pattern changes to adjust to the physical demands placed on the body. With stage fright, this principle works in reverse. Your body changes your breathing pattern in anticipation of a needed physical demand which does not exist. You begin breathing in a shallow manner, pulling more oxygen into your body, and changing the oxygen content in your blood stream. The result: shaking hands, feet, knees, legs, plus dizziness, disoriented feelings, and voice problems.

The solution is to simply become aware of your breathing pattern. Once you realize that you are taking in too much air, simply force yourself to breath slowly, deeply, and normally. The bad news about breathing patterns is they can cause many problematic symptoms. The good news is you can control your air intake at will, thus keeping your body on an even plane.

3. *Distraction Method:* The final method for controlling stage fright is the **distraction method.** Remember what happens during fear: your subconscious and your conscious both focus on the danger. Since there is no physical danger during a public speaking situation, your conscious mind begins to focus on the fear symptoms (heart rate, sweating, shaking, etc.). As your conscious mind worries about these symptoms, your subconscious mind continues to react and increase the symptoms. In short, you worry about the fear, thus creating more fear. As you can see, this is a vicious cycle. What you want to do is use your breathing and burning energy techniques while distracting your conscious mind from the problem. This way, that mental circus is interrupted, and your fear symptoms will begin to decrease. Visiting with audience members, thinking about your speech, or reviewing your notes

are all good distraction methods. Some people prefer to count the bricks in the wall, memorize the feeling of the chair arm, or even sing to themselves! Basically, use whatever distraction method works for you. Remember that during fight or flight, your mind wants to focus entirely on the fear, so distraction will not be easy. Just remember that you are in control and you can force yourself to think about other things.

Common Stage Fright Symptoms

Now that we have discussed three major ways to control stage fright, let's look at a list of stage fright symptoms (Figure 28). I have listed every basic stage fright problem that may affect a speaker. The point of this list is not to scare you or make you think about what might happen. I believe in this rule — an enlightened person can react in an enlightened way. So if you are aware of the possible symptoms you may experience on the day of your speech, you will not be surprised if some of these affect you. The good news about stage fright symptoms is they are not harmful to your body, and they will disappear.

Each symptom listed in the figure is followed by an explanation of the cause and a solution for the problem. Also, a star (*) denotes that the symptom is very common and experienced by almost all people. You may have been in situations in the past where you reacted to stage fright, and you may recognize some of the symptoms. Most people's symptoms are fairly repetitive, so if you have had any of these problems, you will most likely experience them again. Pay special attention to the solutions for those problems.

Figure 28 examines the major symptoms of stage fright. Keep in mind that none of these symptoms are dangerous or damaging to your body. Keep the solutions to each in mind so that you are ready to combat the problems should they arise.

There are some rare instances of extreme stage fright which turn into **panic.** Panic will usually cause two problems. First, panic usually causes a person to become so confused and disoriented that he or she cannot function. Second, fainting spells are common with panic. You should keep two points in mind. First, this rarely happens, and second, should you experience this problem, remember that you are still in control. Even if you have to suspend your speech for a few moments until you recover, your audience will forgive you, and you will be able to give the speech.

Again, I am not mentioning these problems to scare you, but to prepare you. An effective speaker realizes that many problems can arise with stage fright, and an effective speaker knows how to react and cope with those problems.

Finally, there are a few "absolutely do not do this" rules you need to understand. First, never refer to the stage fright problems you are experiencing during the speech. For example, you may have heard a speaker who said, "I'm very nervous about this speech, but here it goes...." Your audience probably knows that you are a little nervous since most people are during a speech, and these kinds of comments completely distract your audience from your speech. Next, never call attention to any problems you are experiencing. Try to avoid rubbing your hands together or wiping your forehead or doing anything that will distract your audience and cause them to think about you instead of what you are saying.

Stage Fright Symptoms

Symptom	Cause/Solution
1. *Shaking Legs or Hands	**Cause:** Adrenaline and other chemicals have given you more energy than your body needs, and irregular breathing has disrupted your blood circulation. Basically, your body is super-charged for fight or flight, which you do not need in a speaking situation. **Solution:** Take several, slow deep breaths and use the tension/relaxation exercise.
2. *Rapid Heart Beat	**Cause:** Adrenaline and other chemicals speed up the heart rate for a fight or flight response. **Solution:** Breath slowly and deeply. Begin thinking about your speech to distract your mind from the problem.
3. *Shallow or Irregular Breathing	**Cause:** With rapid heart beat the body demands more oxygen. **Solution:** Use the breathing method discussed in the last section.
4. *Shaking Voice or Cracking Voice	**Cause:** Irregular breathing. **Solution:** Deliberately slow down your speaking rate. This usually helps control the voice.
5. Stomach/ Intestinal Pain or Noise	**Cause:** Contraction of muscles to prepare for fight or flight. **Solution:** Generally, you can just ignore this symptom. Your audience will not know this is happening and it will not affect your performance.
6. *Dry Mouth or drinking excessive amounts of water.	**Cause:** Accelerated heart rate and adrenaline tends to pull moisture from the mouth and even the eyes. **Solution:** You may want to chew gum until people begin arriving at your speaking event, then discard it. If the symptom continues, you may want to try a mint, but do not begin eating candy (candy may increase the symptom).

Stage Fright Symptoms (cont.)

7. Dizziness   **Cause:** Constricted blood flow to the brain and irregular breathing.
                        Solution: Breathing exercises.

8. Red Splotches   **Cause:** Irregular blood flow to the outer layers of the skin caused
    on the Neck   by adrenaline. This symptom is almost exclusively found in
    and Upper   women, for some unknown reason.
    Chest   **Solution:** There is no way to avoid the skin discoloration, and
                        your audience may notice. Wear clothing that covers the upper
                        chest area and lower neck if possible.

9. Stuttering   **Cause:** Accelerated brain activity. This symptom is more com-
                        mon in men than women.
                        Solution: Deliberately slow down your speaking rate and control
                        your breathing rate.

10 *Sweating   **Cause:** Rapid heart rate raises body temperature, thus causing
                        sweating.
                        Solution: Try to ignore it as much as possible. Do not call atten-
                        tion to the problem by constantly wiping your forehead.

11. Chest Pain   **Cause:** Constriction of chest muscles and irregular blood flow.
                        This symptom mostly happens to men.
                        Solution: Ignore the problem. It is not dangerous to your health
                        and will disappear once you calm down. Obviously, chest pain is
                        a major symptom of heart disease. Chest pain from fear is actual-
                        ly in the chest muscles, not the heart, and will last a very short
                        amount of time. If you have continuous chest pain, see a doctor.
                        Never assume that regular chest pain is due to nerves.

Figure 28. *Stage fright symptoms.*

Again, let me say that this chapter was meant to be an encouragement as you become a more effective public speaker. Realize that stage fright is normal and common; there are specific ways to cope with it. Use the principles we have discussed in this chapter to guide you through your feelings of fear. Also, simply realize that you are going to be okay and *the fear itself is usually worse than what is causing the fear.* As we have learned, the way to solve problems is to anticipate them before they happen, and that is what we have done in this chapter.

CHAPTER TWELVE

Dress for Success

The Florentine statesman and writer, Machiavelli, said, "Men in general judge more from appearances than reality," and we all know the saying, "whatever you do, look the part." Both of these statements are very important for public speakers. You might think, "I already know what I am going to wear when I present my speech, so I'll just skip this chapter." But read on. You might be surprised by what you will discover.

In fact, a person's appearance has great importance in his or her daily activities. Just show up for a job interview in shorts and a t-shirt and see what happens! From our social lives to our occupations, our appearances communicate information about us, and appearance is actually a communication behavior in itself.

In Chapter Nine, we discussed the fact that nonverbal communication includes any type of communication that is not language. In Chapter Nine, we only focused on nonverbal communication that is behavioral — in other words, nonverbal communication that is performed by the body. However, there are also nonverbal communication factors that are not actually behavioral. Many nonverbal communication factors depend on with whom and with what you associate. Other people make judgments about you by where you live, your job, your friends — and yes, your appearance.

Appearance communication is one type of nonverbal communication that has actually gained a lot of attention from researchers over the past 30 years. Frequently, we stereotype people according to their choice of clothing and style. We may label someone as a cowboy, a gang member, a city slicker, as well as a host of others, all according to dress and style. But appearance communication is actually more complicated than just simply the classification of certain people into certain groups. In fact, your appearance has the power to produce **feeling tone** — the positive or negative feelings that people have about others. This chapter explores the basics of appearance communication and examines your choice of clothing and style for a public speaking setting.

Before we get started, let's discuss an important question. When I talk about appearance communication in a public speaking setting, someone usually says, "Shouldn't I just look the way I normally look? Why should I try to be someone I am not? After all, I want to seem real to my audience." This is an important issue and a very valid question. In this chapter, I am going to strongly suggest certain clothing, hair, makeup, and jewelry that you should and should not wear. Some of my advice may conflict with your choice of clothing and style that you wear on a day-to-day basis. Now let's talk about the question — should you wear what you normally wear? The answer is most likely no. Let's consider some fundamental "truths."

• Clothing and styles, no matter what kind, are appropriate only in certain situations. All of us, depending on our ages, cultural groups, backgrounds, and personal tastes have certain types of clothing and styles that we are most comfortable with and most frequently wear. For example, I am most comfortable wearing blue jeans and a t-shirt, but this clothing style is only appropriate in informal settings. If I am at work, a meeting, church, or giving a speech, blue jeans and a t-shirt are simply not appropriate clothing choices. The same can be said for a business suit — it is appropriate for formal settings but not for a day at the park. So, simply realize that there is no "all purpose" clothing. Certain clothing is appropriate in certain situations.

• Clothing or certain style choices do not define who you are as a person. Unfortunately, many people feel that their clothing or style is an accurate depiction of their beliefs, thoughts, feelings, and self-value. But human beings are simply too complex for our appearances to be accurate expressions of who we are. You are in no way selling yourself short if you change your usual style or clothing choice for a certain situation.

• When you give a speech — you are not on display, but your message is on display. As I have stated many times before, your performance, including your appearance, must be message driven.

So, for your presentation, you may need to alter or completely change how you dress and your style choices to effectively communicate your message, and all public speakers do this to a certain extent. With all of that said, let's spend a few minutes discussing some of the assets of the nonverbal power of appearance communication.

1. *Power and Credibility:* Clothing, as a nonverbal communication tool, is symbolic of the power and even the credibility of a person. Although clothing does not actually make a person more powerful or credible, certain types of clothing are symbolic of these qualities. Depending on your choice of clothing and style, people will automatically assume certain things about you. We'll develop this idea later in the chapter.

2. *Respect:* Indeed, the clothing we choose to wear can demand the respect of other people. Consider this example, or you may even try this as an experiment. Walk into an automobile dealership wearing your favorite "Saturday work around the house" clothes and visit with a salesperson briefly about buying a car. A few days later, return in business clothes and speak to the same salesperson. You may discover that you are taken much more seriously about purchasing

a car in your business clothes. Of course, the salesperson doesn't think, "Since this person is wearing business clothes, he must be serious about buying a car," but subconsciously, the salesperson may have more positive feelings about a potential sale. The simple fact is that certain clothing demands respect. In a public speaking setting, your appearance can help demand respect from the audience members. This is a big plus in winning them over to your side — even before you begin speaking.

3. *First Impressions:* Making a good first impression has become a sort of buzz phrase over the past several years, and rightly so. It takes a lot of work on the part of a public speaker, or anyone else for that matter, to overcome a negative first impression, and since first impressions are primarily derived from a person's appearance, the importance of appearance communication is obvious. In Chapter Nine, we discussed your walk to the podium, and even practiced walking to the front of the room, although this isn't actually part of the speech. A confident walk creates a positive first impression, and the right clothes also create a positive first impression.

Now that we have discussed the importance of appearance communication, let's begin to talk about some specifics. First, let's look at some general guidelines about appearance communication, then we'll focus individually on the appearance and clothing of men and women. The following guidelines should be kept in mind at all times as you plan to dress for success.

1. *Always look professional:* Even if you are not what we call a "professional" in the work force, always dress in a professional manner. The clothes that you wear out on the town on Saturday night are probably not appropriate for a speech.

2. *Always wear formal clothing when you give a speech:* If you work in a setting that allows a casual appearance, a speech is not the time to wear casual clothing, even if the clothing looks nice. This does not mean that you have to wear a tuxedo, but you are better to err on the side of being over-dressed rather than underdressed.

3. *Always wear conservative clothing or styles:* This idea includes many factors which we will discuss in detail, but in general, avoid extreme colors, patterns, or unusual tailoring in your clothing - always choose dark colors and patterns over bright colors or loud patterns. The same can be said for your hair, makeup, jewelry, or other accessories.

4. *Consider wearing a red accessory:* Study after study has proven that red is a power color. A red tie or red accessory for a dress is always a good move on your part. Although your speech will not be a failure if you do not wear red, you should at least consider the fact that red subconsciously communicates power and credibility.

Appearance Communication for Women

Before we consider some specific suggestions about appearance communication for women, we should examine one important issue. There is a fundamental difference in communication appearance depending on the speaking setting. As we noted in Chapter One, a speech and a presentation differ in that a presentation is usually given to a specific group for a specific purpose and is usually less formal.

If you are giving a presentation to a group of people that you know or work with on a day-to-day basis, you should dress in a similar manner and fashion as this group normally sees you. If you work in a setting that allows very casual dress, you might want to wear clothing that is somewhat more dressy than you usually wear. The basic point is that you do not want to radically change your appearance with people who see you on a daily basis —this may actually be more distracting.

If you will be speaking to a group that you know or work with, continue to read, paying close attention to the sections on jewelry, makeup, and style, but you will have to make a final judgment about your clothing. If you will be giving a speech to a group of people whom you casually know or do not know at all, you will want to pay careful attention to each of the following sections.

1. *Clothing:* As a general rule, you should wear a dress or a business suit. You should strive for a professional appearance and avoid sleeveless or strapless apparel. Also, dresses should be at least knee length. As we already noted, wear darker colors and avoid extreme designs or styles. Keep it basic and keep it professional. Blue jeans or pants are not appropriate for a speaking situation. You never want to wear anything that causes the audience to question your professionalism or credibility.

2. *Accessories:* Of course, you'll have to wear accessories that match and complement your clothing choice, but again, avoid extreme patterns or colors. You should consider wearing the color red, such as a red belt, if possible. You should not wear a hat.

3. *Shoes:* You will need to wear shoes and hose that match your clothing choice, but try to stay with dark colors. Shoes and hose should be conservative and free from excessive designs or prints. Also, you should wear shoes that are comfortable and stable — you do not want to fall down as you walk to the podium!

4. *Jewelry:* Jewelry can be a great problem for female speakers. Since women normally wear more jewelry than men, many women have a hard time leaving the jewelry at home, which is what you need to do. First of all, excessive jewelry is distracting. Remember that your only purpose for giving a speech is to communicate a message. You do not want the audience to pay more attention to your jewelry than to what you are saying. You may have a fantastic jewelry collection, but a speech is not the time show it off.

Another big problem with jewelry is lighting. Since most public speaking settings have ceiling lights, floor lights, or even spotlights, the extra lighting will make your jewelry sparkle more than usual, which, once again, will distract your audience. Let's consider some specific points:

- *Rings:* It is a good idea to only wear one ring on each hand. Although many women wear more than two rings, you don't want excessive attention called to your hands.
- *Necklaces:* Wear only one necklace and keep it simple.
- *Earrings:* Earrings are fine, but you should avoid large or dangling earrings — small studs are your best option. Large earrings are very distracting and may even glare under certain lighting.

5. *Style:* Overall, hairstyles and make-up should be conservative. Almost any hairstyle, within reason, is fine, just always ask yourself if your appearance will make you look professional. If you have long hair, you need to pull it away from your face. You also do not want your hair to be able to move a lot or fall into your face.

Makeup should not be excessive, but you probably do not need to change the makeup that you wear on a day-to-day basis. Remember that subtle eye makeup can draw attention to your eyes, and this is a positive move. Lipstick makes you look "polished," but avoid unusual colors. Also, nails should be manicured, but extreme lengths or flamboyant colors tend to attract attention to your hands instead of your message.

Appearance Communication for Men

As noted in the section for women, there is a fundamental difference in appearance communication depending on the type of speaking situation. If you are giving a speech or presentation at your place of business for people that you work with on a day-to-day basis, you should dress in the manner that you normally dress for work. It is not necessary for you to wear a three-piece suit to give a presentation to a group of people that normally see you in a shirt and blue jeans. Since these people already know you, your appearance will not greatly change their impressions of you. If you work in an environment that allows very casual clothing, you might consider wearing a tie, but the major idea is not to radically change your everyday appearance — this may actually distract your audience. If you are speaking to a group of people whom you do not know or do not work with, then read on and follow these tips and suggestions.

1. *Clothing:* As a general rule, you should wear a suit or slacks and a coat when you give a speech. In some instances, slacks and a shirt with a tie are appropriate, but think carefully about your speaking situation before leaving off the coat. Semi-casual clothes, such as blue jeans with a shirt and a tie are not good choices for a public speaker. Choose a suit or slacks and a coat that is dark in color and avoid unusual styles. Etiquette probably dictates that you button your coat when you speak, but this is not necessary if you feel more comfortable leaving your coat open.

2. *Shoes / Socks:* Wear dark dress shoes and socks. The last thing you want to do is call attention to your feet. Also, watch out for static cling. You don't want the embarrassment of your pant leg riding up your leg!

3. *Ties:* Your tie is probably the most powerful part of your clothing, and it is the part of your clothing that your audience will primarily notice. Select your tie carefully, keeping these important points in mind:

- Avoid extremely bright colors or an excessive mix of color. You should consider wearing a tie that at least has a red background — this is your most powerful color.
- Wear a tie with a basic pattern or print. Since tie styles change every year or so, you'll have to make a judgment call on the print. But the basic rule to remember is to wear something conservative.
- Avoid ties that have writing or pictures on them. This tends to distract your audience from your message since the audience members may try to read or see the picture on the tie.

4. *Jewelry:* When giving a speech, there is a simple rule about jewelry — less is more. Remember that your speaking setting may have additional ceiling lights or even a spotlight focused on you. This tends to make your jewelry sparkle and it distracts your audience. As a general rule, avoid wearing necklaces and only wear one ring on each hand — you do not want to attract excessive attention to your hands. One final point about jewelry concerns earrings. Many males, especially in the younger generations, now wear earrings. If you wear earrings, I strongly encourage you not to do so when you give a speech. Some people find earrings on males inappropriate and unprofessional, so your best move is to simply not wear an earring.

5. *Style:* With any hairstyle, the basic rule again is to be conservative. If you have long hair, you need to pull it back from your face. Do not do anything that makes you appear less than professional or distracts your audience. Facial hair is fine — just make sure your appearance is neat and trim. You should not wear a hat.

This chapter focused on appearance communication and its importance in a public speaking setting. You should select your choice of clothing and accessories, carefully considering the information that you have read in this chapter. Remember that the clothing and appearance you choose to communicate can give you an instant edge for your speech. Your appearance can make you more credible, believable, and create a positive first impression, and these factors will help communicate your message.

CHAPTER THIRTEEN

Little Things that Make a Big Difference!

It's often the little things in life that make the greatest difference, and the same is true for public speaking. You have written your speech, you have worked on a number of exercises, you are currently practicing your speech, and you have planned your wardrobe. But there are a few simple, yet very important, issues you should understand because these little things can cause you great problems when you perform.

This chapter examines four small issues that may greatly impact the success of your speaking event. In fact, you may have been wondering about these issues as you have read this book. Let's take a look at these to further prepare you for your speaking event.

Using Microphones

Depending on your speaking event, the size of the room, and the number of people who will attend, you may have to use a microphone. At first glance, using a microphone may seem easy. After all, you simply put your mouth close to it and speak. Right? Wrong. Unfortunately, many speakers spend much time and work developing their speeches only to have an ineffective delivery because of a microphone. I do not want this to happen to you!

First, you should decide if you will or will not use a microphone. Often, a microphone will be provided for a public speaker, even when one is not needed. If you are speaking to a group of 40 or fewer people in a conference-sized room, you probably will not need a microphone. Even if you do not need a mike, one may be provided for you, but do not feel as if you are under any obligation to use the mike if you do not need it. The less equipment you use, the fewer complications you will have. If you are speaking to a larger group and a mike will be necessary, consider these important points.

1. *A microphone is not a replacement for your vocal performance.* We discussed this idea in Chapter Eight. Do not depend on a piece of machinery to provide you with an effective vocal performance — it will not happen. For the most part, a microphone simply projects the sound put in to it. In other words, a microphone will not enhance the quality of your voice. Some microphone systems, such as the ones professional singers use, actually help enhance the sound

of the voice. Unfortunately, as a speaker, you will probably not have the luxury of using one of these. Many times, speakers depend on a mike to make them sound good, but you need to prepare for your performance as if you will not use a microphone. Continue to practice your vocal delivery skills discussed in Chapter Eight.

2. *Adjust microphone position before you begin speaking.* Most microphones on a podium contain an adjustable neck that can be positioned according to your height. If you are not using a podium, your microphone should be on an adjustable stand. If possible, place the microphone in the proper position before your audience arrives. If other people will use the microphone before you, you will have to adjust the mike after you walk to the podium. Either way, you want to make sure that the mike is positioned at the proper height before you begin your speech. Do not begin speaking, then pause to make microphone adjustments. This makes your speech very ineffective since moving the microphone calls the audience's attention to the equipment rather than to your speech.

3. *Do not tap or blow on the microphone.* This is a common practice that is very irritating to the audience. If you need to test the mike volume, do so before the speaking event begins. Remember the importance of first impressions. Tapping or blowing on the mike does not make a good first impression with your audience.

4. *The microphone should be about 5 inches from your face.* If you are going to use a microphone, then *use the microphone.* In other words, if you need a mike, make sure that you are close enough. Generally, depending on the type of microphone, your mouth should be about five inches from the mike. If you are further away than this, the mike may not carry the sound of your voice effectively. However, you do not want to stand too close to the mike — this may distort your voice and cause mike feedback. If possible, practice with a microphone a few times before your speech so that you will be familiar with distance.

5. *Do not let the microphone block your face or inhibit your eye contact.* Try to keep the mike and the neck extension below face level so that the audience can clearly see your face. Also, try to ignore the microphone as much as possible. Do not make eye contact with it or do anything that causes you to distract your audience.

6. *Be careful with word pronunciations.* Words that begin with a "p," "th," or similar sounds tend to make microphones "pop." Try to make these sounds a little softer when you speak, and of course, practicing with a microphone will greatly benefit you.

In summary, if you can give your speech without a microphone, do so. You will avoid many potential problems. If you must use a mike, follow the general guidelines above. Chapter Fourteen will discuss how to handle microphone problems or complications, should they arise.

Using a Podium

When I begin teaching a new group of speech students, they always want to stand behind a podium when they give their first speech — and I never let them. Why? A podium is a lot like a baby's pacifier. It is a security blanket that even many experienced speakers never learn to perform without. In many circumstances, they are necessary and quite useful, but overall, I am not a believer in using a podium. Here's why:

In the past couple of chapters, we have discussed how we communicate power and credibility to an audience. Our power is communicated through our nonverbal actions such as posture and even our clothing, and every speaker should want to appear as powerful and credible as possible. However, podiums have a tendency to somewhat decrease the power of the speaker.

A podium appears to be something that the speaker hides behind, or shields himself or herself from the audience. Although this is usually not true, it's a perception problem. A speaker who does not use a podium — one who does not block himself or herself from the audience — appears more powerful and knowledgeable than one who does. So, if at all possible, do not use a podium, but if you decide to, use the following guidelines.

1. *Do not put your hands on it.* Even if you are using a podium, your hands need to fall to your sides unless you are gesturing or moving note cards.

2. *Keep your posture correct.* One of the problems with podiums is that speakers tend to relax too much. They let their posture get sloppy, and they tend to lean on the podium. Even if the audience cannot see your feet, weak posture will still make you appear less competent and professional.

3. *Check podium height.* If you are a little short, you may need a miniature riser to stand on. Do not let a podium "swallow" you. Some conference rooms now have mechanical podiums that you can adjust to your height, plus control the lighting, air conditioning, and audiovisual equipment — all at the touch of a button.

The Speaking Setting

As we noted in earlier chapters, the **speaking setting** is very important in effectively communicating your message. The idea of speaker setting includes a number of factors including room arrangement, lighting, temperature, and even decor. You should remember that the person or persons who set up a public speaking event are often not public speakers themselves. As the speaker, you can suggest how you want the room arranged, the lighting, the temperature, or just about anything else you might want. Do not be afraid to ask questions or make recommendations to the person in charge of your event.

So if you can influence or control the design of the room, what design is best? Let's take a look at some basic ideas about room arrangement, then we'll consider some examples.

1. *The door needs to be at the back of the room.* This seems like an unnecessary statement, but if you don't check on this, you might be surprised. Depending on the size and shape of the room, keeping the door behind the audience may be difficult. Side doors are common in larger rooms or auditoriums, and people entering or exiting during your speech will cause distractions. If your speaking room has more than one door, try to move traffic through the rear door, or one that is closest to it.

2. *Spotlights or footlights need to be focused on the speaker.* Many rooms, and all auditoriums, have some special lighting to help focus attention on the speaker. Even most conference rooms have small ceiling spotlights that can be used. It's a good idea to inspect these lights before your speaking

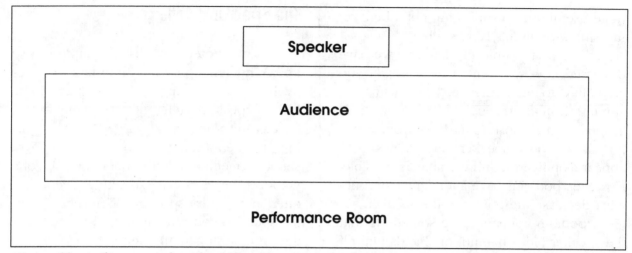

Figure 29. Audience members should be able to easily see the speaker and visual aids the speaker presents.

event to decide what lighting is best for you. You also need to think about visual aids, if you are using them. The lighting is very important and you should definitely test the room lighting before using your visual aids.

3. *The room temperature needs to be slightly cooler than usual.* As the public speaker, it is a good idea to adapt the room temperature to your needs. Remember that public speaking requires a lot of energy, and you will tend to get hot, especially if you have additional lighting on you. If you get hot, you are going to be uncomfortable, and your performance will be affected. Of course, you do not want the room to be so cold that your audience is uncomfortable, but as a safety measure, make the room temperature slightly cool.

4. *Do not use excessive decorations.* If your speaking event will have covered or decorated tables or other decor, you should suggest that the podium or the area in which you will be speaking be free of excessive decorations. One time I watched a speaker who was speaking at a banquet. Behind the podium, there were groups of multicolored balloons. Although the speaker delivered an excellent speech, I was constantly distracted by the bright color of the balloons. Again, this is a small point, but you do not want anything to happen that will distract the audience's attention from your speech.

5. *Room design.* One of the most important aspects of the speaking setting is the room arrangement. Unless you are speaking in an auditorium where the room design is permanent, you should be able to suggest how you want the audience seated.

As a general rule, you want the audience to be in one major block or small blocks that are close together. You should always arrange the audience in a horizontal block rather than a vertical block so that you can keep the audience closer to you. Use the width of the room for chair design. This is especially important if the room is much larger than your audience.

In Figure 29, all audience members will be able to easily see the speaker and any visual aids that the speaker presents. Also, the speaker will be able to easily make eye contact with all of the audience. So, your

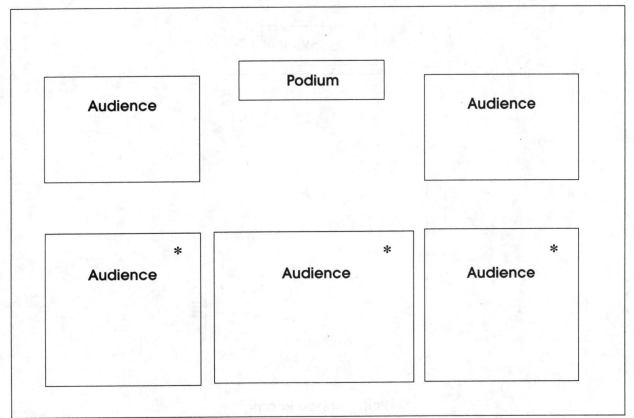

Figure 30. *A room arrangement with two side sections poses unique problems for public speakers.*

most effective design is the most basic — a speaker in front of a grouped audience. Unfortunately, some people who arrange chairs for a speaking event think they should be creative — and this is one instance where creativity is not desired. Take a look at the following examples presented in Figure 30 and 31.

In Figure 30, there are five major blocks of people. The three marked with an asterisk are fine, but the problem begins with the two side sections. Side sections have become somewhat popular because more people can be put into one room, but they are not effective for most public speaking events. First, the speaker has a 180-degree range for eye contact purposes. Not only will the speaker have the front three sections, but he or she will have to make eye contact to the extreme left and right. This makes the speaker's job much more difficult. Second, people sitting in the side sections will be unable to see any visual aids that the speaker uses. Third, if someone in either side section needs to leave the room during the speech, most of the audience will be able to see this person get up and walk out, which distracts them from you. So, this is not a design that you should use.

Look at Figure 31. This is still a one-block audience, but instead of using the width of the room, the audience has been blocked into one narrow unit. This puts the people in the last quarter a long way from

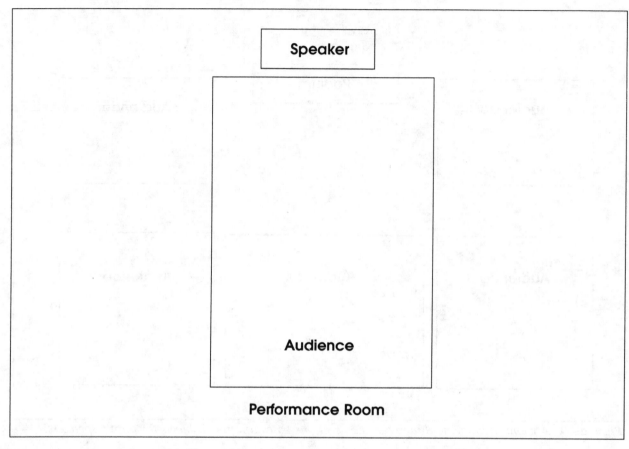

Figure 31. *The audience has been blocked into one narrow unit.*

the speaker or the visual aids. Even if you will be speaking to a smaller audience, you should arrange the audience in a small, wide block instead of a narrow block.

Now let's consider a plan for banquet seating where tables will be used. Take a look at the floor plan in Figure 32.

The black square represents the speaker's podium. At a banquet, there are often side tables for officers or people who are in charge of the event. These side tables are fine, if you are not using visual aids, and you should focus most of your eye contact on the main audience section. Notice that the audience tables are facing the speaker

"end first." This is a preferable arrangement. If the tables face the speaker sideways, then half of the people at each table will have to turn their chairs around to be able to see the speaker. In the arrangement shown in Figure 32, minimal movement from the audience is required.

In summary, keep the following points in mind for seating design:

- Keep the audience close to you. Avoid narrow seating designs that move the audience away from you.
- Try to avoid seating that is on the extreme left or right sides.
- If you are using visual aids, consider

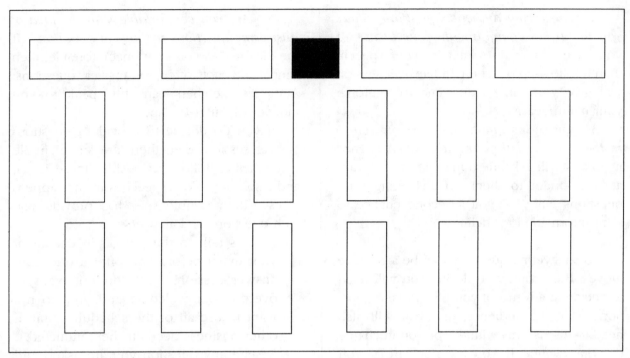

Figure 32. *A floor plan for banquet seating.*

which type of seating design is best for the visual aids. Remember, you want everyone in the audience to be able to see your visual aids.

- If the audience will be seated at tables, make sure the ends of the tables face you.

Answering Questions

Depending on the type of speaking event, your audience may want to ask you some questions after the speech. In very formal situations, such as dinners or banquets, the audience normally does not ask the speaker questions; however, questions may be appropriate in almost any situation. If you are speaking to a smaller group about a specific issue or problem, then you should expect some audience questions. But is a question-answer session really necessary? Let's consider what a question and answer session can do for you and your audience.

1. *Your audience has the opportunity to clarify information they did not understand.* This entire book has basically taught you to effectively communicate information to a group of people. But let's face the facts. No matter how prepared you are, no matter how well you presented your speech, there will still be audience members who didn't catch the whole point. We all understand and perceive information differently, so if you are able to further an audience member's understanding of the content of your speech — even if you presented the information well — then you have done a positive thing.

2. *Answering audience questions allows you to further communicate your ideas.* If you have a strict time limit for your speech, then a follow-up question and answer session will give you some extra time to reinforce your main ideas.

3. *Answering questions will allow you to further connect with your audience.* Audience members will ask questions that are relevant and important to them, so answering their questions will give you a second chance to slant information to them.

So, answering questions can be a positive move. But should you do it? You will need to decide in advance if you plan to take questions from the audience, and you will also need to discuss this with the person in charge of your event. If you are not sure if you should answer questions, then here are a few ideas that will help you make that decision:

1. *Is your speech very general in nature?* If it is, then you probably do not need to take audience questions. The sample topic we used as an example in Chapters Two through Four about active learners probably does not need a question-answer session. The information is very general in nature and the audience would probably not have many questions to ask. Of course, the speaker could still answer questions, if he or she wanted to do so.

2. *Are you trying to teach your audience something or persuade them to do something?* If you are, then you probably need to allow your audience to ask you questions if time allows.

3. *Are you speaking to a small group, such as a group within your place of business?* If you are, then you probably need to provide a question-answer session.

4. *Are you comfortable with the idea of answering questions without preparation?* If the idea makes you very uncomfortable, then simply do not offer to answer questions. Audience members can still speak to you individually after the speech.

If you do decide to provide a question-answer session, then there are some simple guidelines to follow. Consider these ideas, and also refer to the speeches in the appendices. Both sample speeches provide you with questions and answers.

- Always talk to the person in charge of your event before you offer a question-answer session. You do not want to overdo your welcome and you do not want to use all of the scheduled time if other business needs to be conducted.
- Restate any question you are asked and validate it. When you answer an individual's question, you are still speaking to the entire audience — so you want to include them and make sure they all heard and understood the question. Also, you want to make the question important and relevant — even if it isn't — to put the audience member at ease. Pretend that a speaker is giving a speech during a celebration of Earth Day about the benefits of backyard gardening. Consider this example:

Question: I receive a lot of catalogues for mail order plants. The prices seem good, but how about the quality?

Answer: Are mail order houses good places to buy plants? This is a very important question. As a matter of fact, the mail order plant business brings in millions of dollars each year.

In this example, the speaker begins the answer by first restating the question, then validating its importance for all of the audience members.

- Keep your answer short and to the point. You don't want to give another speech for an answer.
- Make sure you simply and clearly answer the question. Let's continue with the example and see how the speaker answered the question:

Question: I receive a lot of catalogues for mail order plants. The prices seem good, but how about the quality?

Answer: Are mail order houses good places to buy plants? This is a very important question. As a matter of fact, the mail order plant business brings in millions of dollars each year. Most mail order houses provide excellent products, quick service, and good prices. I order a number of bulbs and plants through the mail each year. Overall, I have been very pleased with the plants I have purchased, and most mail order houses offer an unconditional guarantee. If you are interested in ordering plants through mail, start out with a small order to see if you are pleased with what you receive.

The answer provided is simple, short, and directly answers the question. The speaker can answer many questions in only a few minutes by using this approach.

Of course, this sounds very easy. Unfortunately, many of the questions you will be asked will be difficult or even unanswerable. Let's consider how to handle challenging questions and solve some common problems.

1. *Redirect unrelated questions.* A common problem with question and answer sessions is that some audience members will have a tendency to ask questions that really do not relate to the main ideas of your speech. Even though these questions are not actually relevant, they can usually be redirected so that they relate to the content. Let's continue with our "gardening" example. Let's say that this speaker focused on backyard vegetables and discussed the importance of gardening for the environment, common types of backyard vegetables, and tips for success as the three main points. During a question and answer session, an audience member asks the following question:

Question: I really like to grow roses. What are your favorite types?

This question does not relate to the content of the speech, since the speech focused on growing vegetables. But the speaker can easily redirect the question. Consider this answer:

Answer: What are my favorite types of roses? Well, I enjoy all types of roses, and the rose is probably the most popular type of flower in America. Although we have focused on vegetable gardening today, any type of gardening is beneficial to our environment. So if you really enjoy flowers, then grow a backyard full of flowers. Thanks for bringing up this important point.

With this answer, the speaker restates the main question, adequately answers the question, relates the question to the main focus of the speech, and validates the question. This answer will satisfy the audience without embarrassing the person who asked the question. When you receive an unrelated question, keep the following points in mind:

- Do not embarrass the person who asked the question in any way.
- Restate and validate the question.
- Quickly answer the question, if possible.
- Relate the question to the main content. Even if the question is really "off the wall," you can still relate it to your content in some way.

2. *If you are asked a several part question, answer generally and stick to the main point.* Sometimes an audience member will ask a series of questions, which may or may not be related, all wrapped into one question. Consider this example:

Question: I have read that some pesticides may cause cancer and other illnesses. Is this true, and if so, what are some of the possible illnesses and what can we do to avoid them?

This is actually a series of questions put together, and the speaker could talk about all of these for the next 30 minutes and still not adequately answer all of the questions. So, the speaker chooses to answer the question in this manner:

Answer: Are pesticides dangerous and how can we avoid them? This issue has received a lot of attention over the past several years. Current research shows that excessive pesticides may cause illnesses and even environmental harm. Since one of the positive aspects of backyard gardening is to strengthen the environment, you should try to avoid pesticides as much as possible. If you begin to have a serious pest problem, there are a number of books available about natural pest control that is environment friendly. Read some of these books — you might be surprised by what you will discover.

With this answer, the speaker provides a general answer to cover the bulk of the question series. The speaker restates the main questions, validates the questions, provides brief answers, and even encourages the audience to educate themselves on the issue.

3. *If you do not understand a question, try to restate the question, then ask for clarification.* Sometimes an audience member may have a very good question, but becomes nervous or confused as he or she asks it. If you do not understand a question, try to restate it, then ask for clarification. Do not embarrass the audience member. Consider this example:

Question: The back of my house is in full sun...and my tomatoes usually do well, but I'm not sure about other plants besides the tomatoes.

Answer: You are asking which plants grow well in full sun — correct?

With this response, the speaker restates what he or she believes is the question, then asks for clarification. If the speaker is right, the audience member will probably nod, and the speaker can answer the question. If not, the audience member has a chance to restate the question. Once you have the accurate question, remember to validate the question and provide a brief answer.

4. *If you do not know the answer to a question, be honest.* Just because you are speaking about a certain subject, do not feel

that you have to know everything about the subject. Even experts on certain topics are sometimes stumped by certain questions. If you do not know the answer, simply restate the question, then tell the audience that you are not sure of the answer. Do not make up an answer. You may fool them for the time being, but when an audience member discovers that the information you provided was inaccurate, he or she will call into question everything you said. So, be honest. Also, a positive move you can make is to ask the questioner to leave his or her name and address with you. Then, look up the answer and write a brief letter explaining the answer. This is a very warm and friendly act on your part, and your audience will be appreciative.

If you offer to do this, however, make sure that you write to the audience member.

In this chapter, we have discussed four small issues that could affect your performance as a speaker. Remember, if you are using a mike or podium, you should try to practice with those items, you should plan your room arrangement carefully with the person in charge of your event, and talk to that person about providing a question-answer session. Also, present your speech to some of your family or friends and practice answering their questions. A prepared speaker is an effective speaker. Now let's move to Chapter Fourteen where we will discuss and solve some common problems public speakers may face.

Common Problems

Murphy's Law tells us that if anything can go wrong, it will. We probably shouldn't be that pessimistic, but no matter what we do, we should anticipate problems — and public speaking is no exception. What should you do if...the lights go out, an audience member drops a glass, the microphone quits working, your visual aids fall onto the floor?

In this chapter, we are going to examine a number of common problems that public speakers frequently have to contend with. As I stated in Chapter Eleven, the way to solve any problem is to anticipate the problem, then have a solution planned — just in case. No matter how hard you have worked and no matter how prepared you are, problems may arise. Fortunately, in a public speaking setting, there are ways to alleviate or at least control any problem that may occur.

Let's begin by first considering a few basic truths about you and your audience when problems arise. Often, a speaker's attitude and perspective about his or her audience stems from nervousness and a lack of self-confidence, rather than reality. By accepting these simple truths, you will greatly help your presentation should a problem arise.

1. *We live in an imperfect world and your audience knows this.* Public speakers sometimes believe that their presentations must be perfect or the audience will lose all respect for them. This is simply not true. If you experience a problem, whether great or small, your audience wants to help you. Audiences do not like to see a speaker fail.

2. *The problems a speaker may experience usually do not seem as great to the audience as they do to the speaker.* Again, audiences tend to be sympathetic. If a problem arises, the audience will not automatically stop listening to you.

3. *The audience will mirror your behavior.* In other words, if you do not make a problem out to be a big deal, your audience will not either. If you make a problem seem to be catastrophic, your audience will also. So, do not overreact to a problem, and your audience will not over react.

Now that we have examined these three truths, let's look at a list of specific problems that commonly affect speakers and their presentations. I have divided these problems into two main sections: equipment problems and presentation problems.

Equipment Problems

In other chapters, I have mentioned a number of times that a public speaker should never depend on equipment for an effective presentation — and rightly so. Of all the problems I have experienced while giving speeches, **equipment problems** rank number one. Sometimes it seems that technical equipment has a mind of its own. No matter how many times it flawlessly works during practice, equipment always seems to fail during the actual speaking event. Since this is such a serious and common problem, let's consider some of the common types of equipment speakers may use, the problems that can arise, and how to solve those problems.

1. *Microphone Problems:* Out of all the possible complications that may arise, microphones seem to most frequently break down or cause problems. We have already had a lengthy discussion about using mikes, but let's spend a few minutes discussing some common problems.

For the most part, there are two common problems with microphones — failure and distractions. As we learned earlier, you need to thoroughly test the mike you will be using before you speak. Test the sound level and the quality of the sound it is producing. If it does not sound right, get someone to help you adjust it. Do not assume

that it will work properly once you are at the podium. If your microphone completely stops working during your speech, follow these guidelines:

- *If you are speaking to a smaller group that can hear you without a mike, quickly turn off your mike, fill your lungs with air, and project your voice.* Do not stop speaking to do this or break the flow of your speech to comment on the problem. Your audience already knows what has happened, so don't call more attention to it. Do not wait for someone to correct the problem. Once the mike fails, turn it off and present your speech without it.

- *If you are speaking in a situation where you must have a microphone, stop speaking and ask the person in charge of the event or someone near you to correct the problem.* If most of your audience will not be able to hear you without the mike, then there is no point to continue speaking. Once the mike problem is corrected, you should say something like, "I believe the problem is now corrected. We were talking about...," then continue with your speech. I personally recommend that you do not apologize for the problem. There is simply no need for you to make a brief apology speech before you continue. The problem has been corrected so do not continue to draw the audience's attention to it.

A more common problem with microphones is distraction noise, such as distortion, feedback, popping noises, or other sounds. If this happens, follow these guidelines:

- Move your head slightly away from the

mike. You may be too close to it. Continue your speech without making comments about the problem.

- If the problem continues, try to ignore it if possible. If the problem is minor, simply ignore the problem and do not draw attention to it.
- If the problem is great enough that it is affecting your communication ability, stop speaking and follow the same guideline given previously.

2. *Media/Visual Aid Problems:* As stated earlier, the more media products or machinery you use, the more likely you are to experience technical problems. As with microphones, it is vitally important that you allow yourself enough time before the speech to set up your equipment and thoroughly test it. Most potential problems can be solved by carefully setting up your equipment and slowly testing it before the speaking event. If you do experience a problem, follow these basic guidelines:

- *You must not depend on visual aids for your presentation success.* We discussed this idea in earlier chapters. Your speech should be written and planned in a way that you could present it without visual aids.
- *Choose the road of least distraction if a problem arises.* Let me give you an example. Once, when I was delivering a speech for a contest, the air conditioner vent began blowing my poster illustrations off the tripod. In all of the confusion, my visual aids became out of order and turned upside-down. I paused, quickly picked up the visuals, placed them on the stand, and continued the speech. As I used the visuals, I correct-

ed order and placement problems. I never commented on the problem during the speech, and I did not act like there was a major problem. I delivered the speech and still received good scores from the judges. Although a speaker never wants something like this to happen, an effective speaker will contend with problems while keeping the audience's attention focused on the speech content. Obviously, if a problem arises, try to correct the problem, but do not call any more attention to the problem than necessary.

- If you are using a piece of machinery that fails, such as a video player, OHP, or slide projector, pause and try to quickly correct the problem. If you cannot correct the problem, continue your speech without the visual aids. Do not make your audience wait for 10 minutes while you try to correct a problem — this does too much harm to your message.

3. *Platform Problems:* If you will be speaking on a platform or riser of some kind, you should thoroughly check the platform before your speaking event. Most platforms are temporary and simply put together before a speaking event. Of course, the likelihood of a platform collapsing is rare, but some are more stable than others. Walk on the platform, checking to see if it is stable or if it makes a lot of noise. I remember giving a speech on a bad platform at a banquet a few years ago. At first, the platform seemed stable, but as I began speaking, I noticed that the floor was beginning to bow under my weight because of a weakness in the plywood. I ended up having to "hug the podium" to stay off the weak spot. If you should experience

any kind of platform problem, try to compensate for the problem while continuing with your speech. Your audience will probably not even notice.

4. *Building Problems:* Although you will seldom have a problem with the actual room, airconditioners can cause a public speaker some problems. When you arrive at the building on the day of the speech, look for the air conditioner vents in the ceiling of the room. If you are using visual aids, try to set them up in a place where the air is not directly blowing on the visuals. Also, check the podium area. You do not want a strong vent blowing on you when you speak. As the old saying goes — an ounce of prevention is worth a pound of cure.

Presentation Problems

As a speaker gives a speech, a number of **presentation problems** may arise. The good news about presentation problems is you can normally control them with some ease. Let's consider the basic problems and the solution for each one. Some of these ideas overlap from issues we discussed in earlier chapters.

1. *Stumbling:* If you begin to stumble over words so that your delivery becomes choppy, slow down your speaking rate. You are probably speaking too quickly.

2. *Stage Fright:* Do not call attention to any stage fright problems you may experience. Most of the time, your audience will not notice.

3. *Dropped Note Cards:* If you drop your cards or they become out of order, stop and correct the problem. Do not try to wade through your speech without cards. Do not make excessive apologies or excuses to the audience. Simply correct the problem and continue.

4. *Audience distraction:* If there is some kind of audience distraction, such as a crying baby, slow down your speaking rate until the problem is resolved. This will help your audience stay focused on you. Do not call attention or make comments about the problem.

Heckling

One final **presentation problem** we should address is heckling. This happens when an audience member interrupts your speech to make a comment or disagree with something you said. This problem is extremely rare. In fact, you have probably never even heard a live heckler — but if you are doing any kind of political speaking or if you are speaking about a very controversial issue, it could happen. Let's consider how to control a heckler with three easy steps.

1. *Pause:* If someone interrupts your speech, pause and look at the person. Remember that you are the one in power, and audience members respect that power — even a heckler. Most speakers want to speed up their delivery when heckled, but this is the opposite of what you should do. By pausing, you acknowledge the interruption and also cause the audience to acknowledge the problem. After a brief pause, while making eye contact with the heckler, continue your speech. This action is usually enough to quiet a heckler when he or she sees that you are not going to play the game.

2. *If the heckler speaks a second time:*

Pause, look at the heckler, then slowly say, "I will be happy to talk to you individually after the speech, but for now, I am going to deliver this speech and you will be quiet." Then continue your speech.

3. *If the heckler speaks a third time, stop your speech and ask the person in charge of the event to remove the heckler from the audience.* Do not continue the speech until the heckler is gone. Do not allow a heckler to continue to interrupt you — three times are too many already. Also, do not begin arguing with the heckler or insulting the heckler. This may be tempting, but when you do this, you lower yourself to the heckler's level. As the speaker, you should be above this kind of inappropriate behavior.

As I already stated, the likelihood of you being heckled is remote in the extreme, but if you are, do not let the heckler shake your confidence, and remember, you are the one in control.

In this chapter we have focused on several potential problems that could affect your speech. Since it is impossible for us to discuss every problem that could occur, let's conclude this chapter with a general list of suggestions that can be adapted to almost any problem.

- If possible, ignore problems.
- Do not call the audience's attention to problems.
- Do not apologize for problems. Try to quickly solve them, then move on.
- Try not to break the flow of your speech or stop speaking if at all possible.
- If you have to stop speaking, remind your audience what you were talking about when you begin speaking again.
- Do not spend a lot of time trying to repair visual aids. Continue your speech without them.
- Remember, you are the one in control.

Now let's move to the final chapter and look at some important ideas for your "big day!"

CHAPTER FIFTEEN

On the Day of the Speech

You have written your speech, you have practiced your delivery skills, and finally, the big day arrives — it's time for your speech! You have a lot of different feelings — some excitement and maybe some fear — but there's nothing you can do because it's all over — right? No. Your speech is not over until you leave the speaking event and go home. Even the day of your speech is still a preparation day. In fact, many speakers do not realize the edge they can give themselves by just following a few simple ideas on the day of the speech. So, let's walk through the day of your speech, taking a close look at some actions you should and should not do.

Pre-Speech Actions

One basic rule you should follow on the day of the speech is to not radically change your normal schedule. Make sure you get plenty of sleep, and wake up at the same time you normally do. The evening before your speech is not the time for a night on the town. If you do not normally take a morning jog, then the day of your speech is not the time to start an exercise program. Try to keep your usual schedule.

Now let's begin looking at some specifics. When you wake up, I strongly suggest that you eat a nutritious, well-balanced breakfast. Even if you will not be speaking until that evening, you are best to get your day off to a healthy start. There are several reasons for this suggestion. First, a good breakfast will give you the physical and mental energy you will need for the speaking event. Remember that a speech requires a great amount of brain power, and you need to feed your brain good food so that you will be as sharp as possible. More than likely, you will be at least somewhat nervous when you speak, and nervousness requires much energy. Your body can only get energy from the food you put in it — so nutritious eating is a must. When I mention this idea to my speech students, I usually get a few questions. Let's consider these important questions and discuss the answers.

1. *I don't eat breakfast. Should I start on the day of my speech?* If you do not normally eat breakfast, you need to train yourself to eat breakfast for about two weeks before the speaking event. This will give your body

time to get used to this change. Remember that you will need more energy for the speaking event than you might normally need, so you need to supply yourself with the energy.

2. *I usually eat doughnuts every morning. Is this okay?* No. Doughnuts and other pastries are very filling, but are basically sugar and fat. You sometimes feel a surge of energy after eating a doughnut, but the energy is sugar induced and will not last long. Plus, doughnuts are simply not good brain food. As with the first question, train yourself to eat a more healthy breakfast for about two weeks before the speaking event.

3. *What should I eat?* I recommend that you eat either whole grain cereals, fruit, toast, bagels, juice, or any combination of these. Do not eat a heavy meal, such as eggs and bacon.

4. *Can I drink coffee?* If you normally drink coffee in the morning, then you should drink coffee on the day of the speech. Try to drink the same amount of coffee that you normally drink or slightly less. As we already stated, you do not want to choose the day of your speech to change your habits.

While we're talking about food, let's go ahead and consider the rest of the day. Quite often, speaking events are arranged around meals. You may be the speaker at a noon luncheon or the after dinner speaker at an evening banquet. No matter what time of the day you are speaking, I recommend that you eat a well-balanced meal about two hours before your speaking event — and nothing else until after your speech. There are two main reasons for this idea. First, your body uses a lot of energy to digest food, especially heavy meals. This is why you often feel sleepy after lunch. If you eat just before your speech, you will decrease your energy level and your brain power. A second reason is nervous energy. If you eat a big meal, then become nervous, you will probably get a stomach ache, or possibly worse. So, you should eat a well-balanced, but not excessive meal, about two hours before your event. If you are speaking at a luncheon or a banquet, you may be expected to eat with the guests. Depending on your culture group, not accepting food that is offered to you may be considered rude. If you feel that you must eat with the guests, take what you are given and eat a very small amount. This will satisfy your guests and not harm your performance. After you finish your speech, you may feel like "eating a horse" — and that's fine. After all, you deserve it!

Another action that speakers should not take on the day of the speech is what I call "the sudden mind change syndrome." Because of anxiety and excitement, you may feel the need to begin making changes. You may feel like you need to mark out parts of your speech, or begin writing new content. Do not do this. You will be successful if you do not make any last-minute changes. Don't start second guessing-yourself — you have already done a good job. Another aspect of the sudden mind change syndrome is your wardrobe. As we discussed in Chapter Twelve, you should plan what you are going to wear in advance of the speaking event, carefully considering the appearance communication ideas we discussed. Unfortunately, many speakers make last-minute changes in their wardrobes just before the speech. The problem with this change is that your first choice was probably best — you made the decision while you were calm. So select what you are going to wear several days before the speaking event, and do not change your mind.

Next, you should collect and carefully check all of your supplies the day before the speaking event. This is particularly important if you are using visual aids. On the day of the speech, you need to check over your supplies once again before you take everything to the speaking event. You might be surprised at the way things seem to disappear at the last minute.

Finally, let's address the issue of practice on the day of the speech. All too often my speech students say, "I had this speech perfect at home. Why did I do so poorly when I performed?" I usually answer this question with another question — "How many times did you practice this morning?" The students might say, "About eight or ten times." There is a point of overkill on practice. You rehearse so many times that your brain begins to get the information confused. You may have experienced this same problem on a test when you were in school. If you cram, you tend to forget it all. The same is true with your speech.

On the evening before your speech, practice your complete performance no more than two times. On the day of your speech, practice your complete speech twice again — and no more. Try to practice about three hours before your speaking event, then do not practice again. Yes, you can read over your cards a few times, but do not begin cramming the information. I promise, you will do a better job.

Preparing for the Speech

Now let's move to the hour before your speech. It's a good idea to arrive **at least** one hour early. There are several things you need to do when you arrive, so you will want to have plenty of time. Let's take a look at what you should do during the hour before your speech begins, and I recommend that you do these in the order presented.

1. *Check the air conditioning and the seating design to make sure everything meets your approval.* Make sure you check on the location of the air-conditioner vents so that you and your visual aids are not directly under a vent.

2. *Next, if you are using visual aids, slowly and carefully set up your equipment.* After it is set up, check it to make sure everything is in good working order. Make sure your slides are in order, make sure the OHP is adjusted and working correctly, and make sure your posters are in order.

3. *Check and adjust the microphone.* Test it a few times and listen to how loudly it carries your voice. You might even want to say the introduction to your speech so that you will know if the mike is extremely sensitive.

4. *Once you are satisfied with the visual aids, meet with the person in charge of the event and discuss the schedule.* When will you speak? Who will introduce you? Ask again about the time limit and answering questions from the audience, just to make sure.

5. *Once everything is ready and you are satisfied with the physical setting, continue to move around and begin concentrating on your speech.* Do not sit down — this will tend to make you more nervous. As you think about your speech, ask yourself these questions so that you will be focused on the speech content:

- **Why am I talking about my subject?**
- **Why is it important to me?**
- **What do I really want my audience members to know once they leave?**
- **What difference do I want to make in the lives of my audience members?**

6. *When people begin arriving (about 15 minutes before the event begins), go to the rest room.* I know this seems personal, but nervous energy will make you need a rest room break, so take one before the event begins.

7. *As people begin arriving, your mouth may begin getting dry.* This is caused by nervous energy and not because you are thirsty. Do not begin drinking water. The nervous energy will take the water and move it quickly through your system, so you are asking for trouble. If you are extremely thirsty, sip on a small glass of water. Do not begin drinking caffeinated drinks such as coffee, tea, or soft drinks. This will only enhance the nervous energy.

8. *It's a good idea to meet and visit with your audience members.* This will help calm your nervousness, and you will seem more personable to your audience.

9. *Just before the event begins, check your note cards once again for correct order.* Take your seat and do not leave your cards unattended.

10. *If you are feeling nervous, begin the relaxation exercises you learned in Chapter Eleven.*

11. *As the time nears for your speech, keep your attention focused on the podium.* Do not begin scanning your cards or trying to psyche yourself up. Keep your head up and your attention focused.

12. *Keep your posture formal and look at the person who is introducing you.*

13. *It's time to speak!*

As we complete your public speaking training, let me once again offer you a few truths. Out of all the things we have talked about, these few ideas are the core of an effective speaking presentation. Commit these ideas to memory and believe them.

- You have written a speech that is important for others to hear. Be confident.
- Talk "with" your audience — not "at" them.
- You will probably be nervous. This is normal, very common, and something you should expect.
- Let everything you do be message driven. No matter what happens, keep the audience's attention on the message.
- Believe in what you are talking about.

It is my sincere wish that you have a very positive speaking experience. If things do not go quite as well as you had hoped, do not be discouraged. Like all skills, you will get better with each speech that you present. Many of the people who have made a positive impact in our world have been public speakers. You are about to join them. After all, the expression of great ideas and information causes great things to happen. Good luck — and good speaking!

Sample Speeches

In order to give you a complete sample of an informative speech and a persuasive speech, I have created two speakers, public speaking situations, audience analysis notes, and two complete speeches. These speeches incorporate the ideas that we worked on during Chapters Three through Six. I have also included explanatory remarks in parentheses within the texts of the speeches to help you recognize many of the writing techniques we have discussed. At the end of the speeches, I have included sample audience questions and the responses.

Sample Informative Speech

The Speaker: Dr. Alan Merritt, an astronomy professor.
Speaking Situation: This is a speech prepared for a science symposium. The symposium hosts a number of expert speakers as well as many exhibits and demonstrations.
Audience: The audience is made up of science students, high school through college, and other interested individuals from the city. None of the audience members are professional astronomers or scientists, and

the majority of the audience consists of high school students who are on a field trip. The speaker was not provided with any other information about his audience. His most important note, however, is that most of his audience is young, and they are all interested in science issues.
Topic: The planet Mars.
Purpose: To inform the audience members about some of the basic information about Mars. The speaker will use pictures and computer-generated video footage for visual aids. Considering the audience, the speaker will strive to keep the information interesting, yet simple.

The Speech: Mars

Imagine you are sitting in a spaceship. You have been traveling for several months now, and you anxiously begin to land your ship on an alien planet. After touchdown, you step out of the ship onto the foreign landscape. You look at the red, rocky terrain, and you realize that you are the first human to ever set foot on the planet Mars. Sound like a dream? It may not be, for our interest in the planet Mars has only grown during the past hundred years. *[Opens speech with a story that relates to his audience.]*

In fact, the idea of "little green men," or "Martians," has been an important part of all of our imaginations and many of America's movies and books during this century. Many people even feared a Martian invasion, but the truth is that we are the ones who have been invading Mars during the last several decades. In our age of technology, we have learned a lot about the "red planet," as it is sometimes called, and the more we learn about Mars, the more we all want to learn.

So let's spend the next few minutes talking about *[Inclusive pronouns]* this incredible planet. *[Audience clearly understands the speech topic.]* First, let's look at the current information and facts about this planet; second, let's consider the current research plans and goals; and finally, we'll talk about some of the mysteries of Mars that we hope to understand in the coming years. *[Three major topics clearly stated in one sentence and in the order he will discuss them.]*

During the past hundred years or so, there's been a lot of superstitions about Mars, but through technological advancements, we have learned many interesting facts about this planet during the past 30 years. Most of our current information has come from high powered telescopes, the *Voyager* missions which photographed the planet, and the *Viking* probes which landed on Mars and performed soil tests of the alien landscape. Let's consider some of the facts that this research has discovered.

Mars is approximately 142 million miles from the sun and the Martian year lasts 687 days. Mars has two small moons — Phobos and Deimos, both of which look like flying

potatoes and are probably asteroids that were caught in Mars' orbit some time in the past. Mars is only half the size of earth, and because of Mars' small size, the surface gravity is smaller also. If you weigh 200 pounds on earth, you would only weigh about 76 pounds on Mars — sounds like a great diet plan! *[Supporting example.]*

But the low gravity does cause some problems. For one, there isn't much of an atmosphere. Earth's gravity keeps its atmosphere wrapped around it like a coat *[Simile]*, but Mars' gravity allows most of its atmosphere to escape into outer space. Most of the air is carbon dioxide — the gas we all exhale — and you would need a spacesuit to survive on the planet. If you want to get a tan, Mars would not be a good vacation spot. In the summer, the temperature may rise to a cozy 70 degrees. But on an average, the temperature is around zero, and may get as cold as 180 degrees below zero during the winter — certainly not swimsuit weather. *[Audience analysis: most young people enjoy swimming.]*

But the planet surface is rather interesting, and the *Viking* missions of the late 1970s gave us the first pictures of the Martian landscape. The surface of Mars is actually a reddish-brown color and is made up of rocks and desert-like terrain. Its surface is filled with craters, and many of the rocks appear to have come from volcanos. Much to scientists' disappointment, the *Viking* landers discovered no signs of life after performing several soil tests.

The surface does, however, have some interesting features. First, Mars has the longest canyon in the solar system. It's named Mariner Valley and it is 13 times longer than the Grand Canyon — that's about the length of America. *[Qualifying example.]* Mars also has four gigantic volcanos. The first, Olympus Mons, has a base of 435 miles and is about 15 miles at the peak — that's three times taller than Mount Everest, the tallest mountain on earth. *[Qualifying example.]* We should note that mountains this tall cannot exist on earth — they would collapse under their own weight because of our gravity. Olympus Mons has a vent crater at its peak of an incredible 50 miles — not something you would want to be near during an eruption! The three other volcanos, Ascraeus Mons, Pavonis Mons, and Arsia Mons are also approximately 190 to 250 miles wide and reach up to 15 miles high.

But these incredible discoveries have only made us more interested in Mars, and there are a number of plans for further research, which brings us to our second topic — the current exploration plans for Mars. *[Transition: leads the audience from the first point to the second point.]* During the 1980s, NASA's primary focus was on the shuttle program, even though Mars remained a top scientific interest. But it would be over ten years before the next space probe would be sent to Mars. On August 21, 1993, the *Mars Observer* blasted off to photograph the planet and perform other experiments. Eleven months after lift-off from Cape Canaveral, the *Mars Observer* arrived near the planet Mars. Unfortunately, the mission turned into a disaster. During a routine operation to prepare for Mars orbit, the craft suddenly fell silent and Earth never regained contact with the craft. According to *Popular Science,* April 1994 *[cites major research source],* investigators believe that the spacecraft exploded during a fuel-mixing opera-

tion, although we have no way of knowing for certain. At any rate, the *Mars Observer* provided us with one black-and-white picture — at a cost of $950 million.

Although the failure of the *Mars Observer* mission has both financial and political implications, the red planet is still a major research interest and plans for future missions continue. Currently, NASA plans to launch the *Mars Environmental Survey Pathfinder* in 1996 for a 1997 arrival to Mars. This mission would send a lander to a selected position on the planet. According to *U.S. News and World Report,* August 23, 1993, the lander will be equipped with a rover — a six-wheeled, 22 pound, remote control explorer that will scout out the surrounding area. The lander will function on the Martian surface for one year and record weather conditions, seismic activity, and the composition of the surrounding landscape as well as providing a multitude of pictures. NASA hopes to eventually send a fleet of landers to the Martian surface.

Of course, the question we all want to know is, "Will humans ever walk on Mars?" Scientists hope so, and the July 25, 1994 issue of *Newsweek* outlined a plan for such a mission. Originally, such a mission was estimated to cost $400 billion — if you placed dollar after dollar, stretching upward, that's almost enough money to reach the sun! *[Qualifying example.]* But Robert Zurbin, an engineer with Martin Marietta Astronautics Group, devised a plan to cut the cost by an impressive $150 billion. Basically, the plan calls for sending a small reactor to the Martian surface to begin creating rocket fuel. This way, astronauts do not have to carry all of the fuel for the return voyage, thus greatly changing the spacecraft and its size.

About a year later, the astronauts would blast off, make the six-month trip to Mars, and land on the planet surface. While on the planet, the astronauts would set up a miniature space station and live on the planet for 500 days. After the exploration, the astronauts would blast off the Martian surface and make the six-month journey home. Sounds easy, right? Well, such a mission is extremely dangerous, and one of the greatest problems is that the astronauts must deal with every crisis on their own. A rescue mission would be impossible. But still scientists are hopeful that one day in the near future this dream will become a reality.

But why Mars? Why are we so interested in this planet? Why do we want so desperately to explore this alien world? The answer is in the unsolved mysteries of Mars, which brings us to our final topic. *[Transition: leads audience from second point to third point.]* Through NASA's space probe research, several fascinating findings have emerged. One of those findings is the polar ice caps on Mars which are similar to Earth's. The southern ice cap is primarily water, while the northern ice cap seems to be made up of frozen carbon dioxide, or dry ice. The ice caps are larger during the winter and smaller during the summer.

Now, ice caps alone do not seem like such a great mystery, but Mars also contains many large and small "canals" which seem to indicate that the planet once had water. Early theorists believed that the canals were actually created by intelligent beings, but later researchers now believe that the many canals on the Martian surface were cut by water, such as our rivers, streams, and lakes. According to *U.S. News and World Report,* August 23, 1993, there is even evidence that

Mars has had widespread flooding at various times in its history. If this is true, the main question of course is, "Where did all of the water go?" This is a question for which we do not have an answer, but it does lead us to the next question. Is there life on Mars, or has there ever been life on Mars?

Although the *Viking* landers failed to detect any signs of life, the possibility of water existing on the planet makes scientists even more excited and interested. Scientists particularly want to search for fossils or any form of plant life on the planet. Of course, we don't expect to find any "little green men" *[relates to opening remarks],* but the possibility of life is a great mystery that scientists definitely want to solve.

Out of all of the planets in our solar system, Mars is one of the most fascinating. *[Transition: leads audience from the speech body to the conclusion.]* Today we have talked about the current information and facts, the future exploration plans, and the mysteries of the planet Mars. *[Restates the three major topics discussed.]* There is still much to be learned about the "red planet," and who knows, maybe it will be some of you — some of our future scientists — who takes the first step onto Martian soil. *[Closing remarks tie directly to opening remarks.]*

Sample Questions

Question: If the *Viking* probes didn't find any signs of life, why do scientists still want to look?

Answer: Why do scientists still want to look for signs of life, even though *Viking* did not find any? This is a good question, especially since space missions are so costly. The

Viking landers only tested the soil in the location that they landed. In other words, the landers could not travel to different locations. Scientists want a more thorough search of the planet before we rule out any signs of life. Just because the landers did not detect signs of life in one location does not mean that the whole planet is void of any life forms. *[Restates the question, validates it, and provides a brief answer.]*

Question: I heard that NASA is planning to send a probe to Venus. Is this true?

Answer: Is NASA sending a probe to Venus? Venus is a fascinating planet, but I am not aware of any research plans that are coming up in the near future. However, Mars is my primary research interest, so I may be mistaken. A quick trip to the library will tell you all about NASA's future space exploration plans. *[Speaker is not sure of the answer, so he answers honestly and provides the audience with a way to find out for themselves.]*

Question: What are NASA's future exploration plans for Mars?

Answer: What are NASA's future exploration plans for Mars? Aside from the *Mars Environmental Survey Pathfinder,* there are no definite plans. However, the manned missions are still a future possibility, and scientists are even considering some international missions where several countries cooperate together in Mars exploration to cut the costs. *[Since the speaker has already discussed the exploration plans in detail, he simply restates the plans and provides another small piece of information.]*

Sample Persuasive Speech

The Speaker: Diane Smith, an environmental expert employed by the state environmental office.
Speaking Situation: The speaker has been asked to speak at the Women's Urban League, a local service organization.
Audience: The audience is composed of approximately 60 female members, ranging in age from 26 to 55. Twenty percent are white-collar workers, 40% are blue-collar workers, 30% are homemakers, and 10% are retired. All of the league members are very active in civic affairs. Almost all of the members perform volunteer work at local schools and hospitals.
Topic: Plastic pollution.
Purpose: The speaker has two major goals. First, she wants to educate the audience about the plastic pollution problems, and second, she wants to persuade the audience members to begin neighborhood plastic recycling programs. The speaker has been given a fifteen minute time limit including audience questions. She will not use any visual aids.

The Speech: Plastic Pollution

Last summer, I was driving down a rural deserted road in a nearby county. As I drove along, I began to notice piles of debris in the ditches. I saw milk cartons, plastic trash bags, old plastic toys, furniture, and many other household items. The trash was simply piled there — as if there were nowhere else to put it. And I have to admit - the sight frightened me. I began to imagine a world that looked like this old deserted road — a world full of discarded trash — a world full of plastic pollution *[parallel structure]*.

In fact, the problem of plastic pollution has become a great national concern, and one that has received a lot of attention *[begins speech with a personal story]*. Many states have even passed recycling laws in an attempt to control plastic pollution. Now do not misunderstand, plastic is one of the most valuable materials we have. We use plastic products every day, and with advances in modern medicine, plastic products are even saving the lives of many people. But with all of the positive aspects of plastics usage, pollution is a formidable problem.

Today, let's spend some time talking about this problem *[clearly states the speech topic]*. First, let's talk about the problem with plastic to understand why it is such a serious pollutant. Second, we'll take a look at the current action people are taking to reduce plastic pollution, and finally, we'll consider how we, as individuals and as a community, can help solve this important problem *[three main points clearly stated]*.

When plastic was first invented many years ago, it was a milestone, and it didn't take long for plastic to change our world *[transition]*. Today, almost every product we purchase has at least some plastic parts — from automobiles, to furniture, to computers, to dishes, to processed food wrappers — the list is virtually endless. And there are many positive aspects of this. After all, plastic is durable, it's inexpensive, it's great for protecting food products, and in so many ways, it makes all of our lives much easier. Just imagine your life without plastic trash bags! But with all of these advantages comes great problems.

So what is the big deal about plastic pollution? Why is it so different than other products? The answer is in the "biodegradability." Webster's Dictionary defines biodegradable as "capable of being readily decomposed by biological means." Simply put, biodegradable products easily "break down" or rot in the natural environment. Let's consider an example.

Let's say that a careless motorist tosses a paper soft drink cup out of the car window. As the environmental elements, such as the sun, rain, and bacteria, begin to work on the paper cup, it will deteriorate, or rot, and become a completely natural part of the environment in about three years. After all, it's made of wood. Now let's say that this same motorist throws a plastic cup out of the car window. Plastic is not a natural part of the environment, and the natural environment does not affect plastic in the same way. Three hundred years from now, the plastic cup will still be here *[supporting example]*! And that is the problem with plastic — it does not biodegrade in a reasonable amount of time.

But what does that really mean? How does the fact that plastic does not biodegrade affect of us? Think of it this way. Picture the inside of your home, and think about all of the plastic products you have and use on a daily basis. Now think about the trash that you throw away every week — think about all of the plastic in your garbage. Your garbage goes to a landfill where it should biodegrade over time — but your garbage is full of plastic. It will not biodegrade in a landfill. Now take your garbage and multiply it by the millions of other people in our world. You can quickly see the problem! Plastic continually takes up landfill space and pollutes our environment.

The pollution has even stretched to the ocean. Congress's Office of Technology Assessment *[cites major research source]* reports that an estimated 100,000 marine mammals die every year from ingesting discarded plastic products or becoming tangled in them. This same office reports that approximately 26,000 tons of plastic are dumped into the ocean by ships, fishermen, and recreational boats every year. And since it doesn't biodegrade, the pollution only gets worse year after year.

But people are not ignoring this important problem, which brings us to our second point, the current action against plastic pollution *[transition]*. In the late 1980s, many industries began to attack the plastic pollution problem. Research in plastic production helped companies create plastic that is more biodegradable, a hopeful creation for plastic trash bags that continually crowd landfills. Unfortunately, this biodegradable plastic did not quite perform as well as we had hoped. Scientists discovered that the biodegradable plastic simply breaks down into smaller pieces, but doesn't actually degrade into the environment. *U.S. News & World Report,* March 26, 1990, *[cites major research source]* reports that true biodegradable plastics will have to be developed from living cells and not petroleum — but these products are a long way from consumer use.

But even though biodegradable plastic isn't our saving answer, many businesses have individually attacked the plastic pollution problem with their products. Many corporations, such as McDonald's, are now wrapping their products in paper and cardboard instead of plastic and styrofoam. Additionally, many companies are now packaging their products in plastic that can be recycled. The "three arrow" symbol has become a common sight to us all!

But these efforts by industry must be helped by the public — and that brings us to our final point — the action, we, as individuals, can take *[transition]*. Fundamentally, we need a grassroots effort to control plastic pollution — and it's not as hard as you might think! First, when you are given a choice, always buy a biodegradable product, such as paper or cardboard. When you are at the grocery store, ask for paper bags instead of plastic. When you are buying a product, try to buy the product in a paper or cardboard wrapping; it's a small effort that is very environment friendly. Second, look around your home and even in your trash and ask yourself how you can use fewer plastic products. Especially examine your kitchen — think about the products that you use on a daily basis and try to substitute some of the those products for paper. Finally, one of the most important actions you can take is to organize a plastic recycling program in your neighborhood. Most cities now have free plastic pickup if residents will simply bag it. All this means is that you have to separate plastic trash from other trash. It's very easy — and on a nationwide scale — it has a big impact. I know that many of you are leaders in your neighborhood, and we need people like you who will be willing to take on this cause *[audience analysis]*.

I encourage each of you to stand up and become a leader in your neighborhood to control plastic pollution *[transition]*. Today we have considered the problem with plastic, the current action being taken against pollution, and how we, as individuals, can help reduce plastic pollution *[restates the three major topics discussed]* by choosing products that are plastic free, reducing plastic consumption in our homes, and encouraging others to recycle plastic by beginning a neighborhood campaign. Our environment must be cared for — and we must reduce plastic pollution for our future generations. Our world doesn't have to become like that old abandoned road — *[interruption]* plastic pollution can be controlled — but it has to begin with each of us. *[relates conclusion to the opening story.]*

Sample Questions

Question: Why is plastic so dangerous?

Answer: Why is plastic so dangerous? That's an important issue we must all understand. As we discussed, since plastic doesn't biodegrade, our pollution problem only gets worse as we add more and more plastic to landfills each year. Additionally, plastic poses a threat to many types of marine animals and wildlife. This is why it is so important that we control our plastic consumption and pollution. *[The speaker discussed this topic in detail, so she restates the question and provides a brief summary.]*

Question: How can we get people in our neighborhoods to cooperate in the recycling program?

Answer: How can you get people in your neighborhood to cooperate in the recycling program? This is a very important issue. One of the best ways you can get cooperation is to educate the people in your neighborhood about the problem. It takes minimal effort to separate plastic trash from other trash, so once people understand the importance, they will usually cooperate.

Another way you can get cooperation is by organizing a children's club in your neighborhood to help the residents carry out the plastic trash and encourage people to participate. Because of programs in schools, children tend to be very environment conscious and are usually willing to help. *[The speaker provides two brief, direct action tactics for the answer.]*

Question: I sponsor a neighborhood program to keep our area clean and pollution free. Can I incorporate a plastic recycling program with the existing program?

Answer: Can you combine a recycling program with other pollution control programs? Absolutely! One of the advantages of plastic recycling is that it will work with existing pollution control programs. Because plastic recycling is so easy, just teach the people in your neighborhood to include plastic recycling in the program you already use. *[The speaker provides a brief answer, reasserting the ease of recycling programs.]*

A Close Look at Three Great Speeches

In order to further your understanding of speech organization, I have selected three famous speeches for us to examine. In these three speeches, you will see a number of the organizational ideas and writing techniques that we discussed in Chapters Three through Six. I have included explanatory remarks in brackets within the texts of these speeches to point out some of the ideas that we discussed.

"Bank Closings: The First Fireside Chat"
Franklin D. Roosevelt

Two days after his inauguration, Roosevelt closed every bank in the nation for a nine-day examination and appraisal of assets. Since no depositor could withdraw, deposit, or even cash a check, Roosevelt decided to give his first radio "Fireside Chat." After examining a scholarly draft of the speech written by the Treasury Department, Roosevelt decided to write his own speech that would clearly communicate to the American public. He strived to make the information simple and to use language that would give the speech a conversational tone, and you will see that he uses the basic speech model that we discussed. This speech was delivered on March 12, 1933.

I want to talk for a few minutes with the people of the United States about banking — with the comparatively few who understand the mechanics of banking, but more particularly with the overwhelming majority who use banks for the making of deposits and the drawing of checks. I want to tell you what has been done in the last few days, why it was done, and what the next steps are going to be. *[Instead of opening the speech with introductory statements, he begins with the major points he will discuss. Because of the fear and concern of the American public, Roosevelt wanted them to know exactly what he was going to talk about during the speech.]* I recognize that the many proclamations from state capitols and from Washington, the legislation, the Treasury regulations, etc., couched for the most part in banking and legal terms, should be explained for the benefit of the average citizen. I owe this in particular because of the fortitude and good temper with which everybody has accepted the inconvenience and hardships of the banking holiday. I know that when you understand what we in Washington have been about I shall continue to have your cooperation as fully as I have had your sympathy and help during the past week. *[Roosevelt praises the audience — this helps develop conversational tone because it makes the address personal.]*

First of all, let me state the simple fact that when you deposit money in a bank, the bank does not put the money into a safe-deposit vault. *[Transition — First point. Roosevelt begins to explain what has happened.]* It invests your money in many different forms of credit — bonds, commercial paper, mortgages, and many other kinds of loans. In other words, the bank puts your money to work to keep the wheels of industry and of agriculture turning around. A comparatively small part of the money you put into the bank is kept in currency — an amount which in normal times is wholly sufficient to cover the cash needs of the average citizen. In other words, the total amount of all currency in the country is only a small fraction of the total deposits in all of the banks.

What, then, happened during the last few days of February and the first few days of March? Because of undermined confidence on the part of the public, there was a general rush by a large portion of our population to turn bank deposits into currency or gold — a rush so great that the soundest banks could not get enough currency to meet the demand. The reason for this was that on the spur of the moment it was, of course, impossible to sell perfectly sound assets of a bank and convert them into cash except at panic prices far below their real value.

By the afternoon of March 3, scarcely a bank in the country was open to do business. Proclamations temporarily closing them in whole or in part had been issued by the governors in almost all the states. *[Transition — Second point. Roosevelt begins to discuss why the banks were closed.]*

It was then that I issued the proclamation providing for the nationwide bank holiday, and this was the first step in the government's reconstruction of our financial and economic fabric.

The second step was the legislation promptly and patriotically passed by the Congress confirming my proclamation and broadening my powers so that it became possible in view of the requirement of time to extend the holiday and lift the ban of that holiday gradually. This law also gave authority to develop a program of rehabilitation of our banking facilities. I want to tell our citizens in every part of the nation that the national Congress — Republicans and Democrats alike — showed by this action a devotion to public welfare and a realization of the emergency and the necessity for speed that it is difficult to match in our history.

The third stage has been the series of regulations permitting the banks to continue their functions to take care of the distribution of food and household necessities and the payment of payrolls.

This bank holiday, while resulting in many cases in great inconvenience, is affording us the opportunity to supply the currency necessary to meet the situation. No sound bank is a dollar worse off than it was when it closed its doors last Monday. Neither is any bank which many turn out not to be in a position for immediate opening. The new law allows the 12 Federal Reserve Banks to issue additional currency on good assets and thus the banks which reopen will be able to meet every legitimate call. The new currency is being sent out by the Bureau of Engraving and Printing in large volume to every part of the country. It is sound currency because it is backed by actual, good assets.

A question you will ask is this: Why are all the banks not to be reopened at the same time? The answer is simple. Your government does not intend that the history of the past few years shall be repeated. We do not want and will not have another epidemic of bank failures. *[Transition — Third point. Roosevelt begins to discuss the next steps.]*

As a result, we start tomorrow, Monday, with the opening of banks in the twelve Federal Reserve Bank cities — those banks which on first examination by the Treasury have already been found to be all right. This will be followed on Tuesday by the resumption of all their functions by banks already found to be sound in cities where there are recognized clearinghouses. That means about 250 cities of the United States.

On Wednesday and succeeding days, banks in smaller places all through the country will resume business, subject, of course, to the government's physical ability to complete its survey. It is necessary that the reopening of banks be extended over a period in order to permit the banks to make applications for necessary loans, to obtain currency needed to meet their requirements, and to enable the government to make common sense checkups.

Let me make it clear to you that if your bank does not open the first day, you are by no means justified in believing that it will not open. A bank that opens on one of the subsequent days is in exactly the same status as the bank that opens tomorrow.

I know that many people are worrying about state banks not members of the Federal Reserve System. These banks can and will receive assistance from member banks and from the Reconstruction Finance Corporation. These state banks are following the same course as the national banks, except that they get their licenses to resume business from the state authorities, and these authorities have been asked by the Secretary of the Treasury to permit their good banks to open up on the same schedule as the national banks. I am confident that the State Banking Departments will be as careful as the national government in the policy relating to the opening of banks and will follow the same broad policy.

It is possible that when the banks resume, a very few people who have not recovered from their fear may again begin withdrawals. Let me make it clear that the banks will take care of all needs — and it is my belief that hoarding during the past week has become an exceedingly unfashionable pastime. It needs no prophet to tell you that when the people find that they can get their money — that they can get it when they want it for all legitimate purposes — the phantom of fear will soon be laid. People will again be glad to have their money where it will be safely taken care of and where they can use it conveniently at any time.

I can assure you that it is safer to keep your money in a reopened bank than under your mattress. The success of our whole great national program depends, of course, upon the cooperation of the public — on its intelligent support and use of a reliable system.

Remember that the essential accomplishment of the new legislation is that it makes it possible for banks more readily to convert their assets into cash then was the case before. More liberal provision has been made for banks to borrow on these assets at the Reserve Banks and more liberal provision has also been made for issuing currency on the security of these good assets. This currency is not fiat currency. It is issued only on adequate security, and every good bank has an abundance of such security.

One more point before I close. There will be, of course, some banks unable to reopen without being reorganized. The new law allows the government to assist in making these reorganizations quickly and effectively and even allows the government to subscribe to at least a part of new capital which may be required.

I hope you can see from this elemental recital of what your government is doing that there is nothing complex, or radical, in the process.

We had a bad banking situation. Some of our bankers had shown themselves either incompetent or dishonest in their handling of the people's funds. They had used the money entrusted to them in speculations and unwise loans. This was, of course, not true in the vast majority of our banks, but it was true in enough of them to shock the people for a time into a sense of insecurity and to put them into a frame of mind where they did not differentiate, but seemed to assume that the acts of a comparative few had tainted them all. It was the government's job to straighten out this situation and do it as quickly as possible. And the job is being performed.

[Conclusion. Roosevelt begins the conclusion by praising the American people.] I do not promise you that every bank will be reopened or that individual losses will not be suffered, but there will be no losses that possibly could be avoided; and there would have been more and greater losses had we continued to drift. I can even promise you salvation for some at least of the sorely pressed banks. We shall be engaged not merely in reopening sound banks, but in the creation of sound banks through reorganization.

It has been wonderful to me to catch the note of confidence from all over the country. I can never be sufficiently grateful to the people for the loyal support they have given me in their acceptance of the judgment that has dictated our course, even though all our processes may not have seemed clear to them.

After all, there is an element in the readjustment of our financial system more important than currency, more important than gold, and that is the confidence of the people. Confidence and courage are the essentials of success in carrying out our plan. You people must have faith; you must not be stampeded by rumors or guesses. Let us unite in banishing fear. We have provided the machinery to restore our financial system; it is up to you to support and make it work.

It is your problem no less than it is mine. Together we cannot fail. *[Concluding lines ask for Americans to come together as a nation.]*

"Speech Introducing Indira Gandhi"
Alfred Hayes

Alfred Hayes, the president of the Economic Club of New York, presented this speech to the members of the club to introduce the speaker, Indira Gandhi, then Prime Minister of India, in the spring of 1966. You will notice this speech follows the model that we discussed in Chapter Five for speeches of introduction.

Our speaker tonight is the head of government of the world's second most populous nation. *[Begins the speech by talking about the speaker's political position.]* She speaks for an ancient country to which we in the West look for much of our heritage of civilization. But more importantly, she speaks for a country which we believe is one of the great hopes of tomorrow's world. Those of us who have visited India have been impressed both by the vastness of its problems and by the importance to the world of their successful solution.

It is no small task to follow in the footsteps of those two brilliant and revered leaders who were in large measure responsible for the emergence of India in this century as a major independent nation. I am speaking, of course, of Mahatma Gandhi and Jawaharlal Nehru, the father of our honored guest. After them, how would India find the leadership needed to sustain it on the path of democracy? Even those who know little about India have the instinctive feeling that the right choice has been made.

It would be presumptuous on my part to try to summarize Mrs. Gandhi's distinguished career, and I know you are impatient to get to the main event of tonight's program. [Begins to focus on the speaker's personal accomplishments.] Most of you have read about Mrs. Gandhi's steady rise to political eminence. Certainly she received the best kind of training for her vast responsibilities: as a militant young activist and disciple of

Mahatma Gandhi in the noncooperation movement; as a student at Oxford privileged to see the best of Western culture and to view India in perspective; as a member and later as a high official of the Indian National Congress; as a participant in all kinds of social work; as Minister of Information and Broadcasting; and as official hostess and unofficial confidante of her illustrious father. In these and other capacities, she achieved a broad understanding of India's goals and India's problems.

While it would be foolish to overlook her debt to a great father — in natural traits, in an awareness of the importance of service and sacrifice, and in exposure to his wise judgements — the striking fact is that Mrs. Gandhi achieved much of her success through her own merit.

If I have not stressed the fact that India's Prime Minister is a woman, it is because she has won recognition as a statesman in full competition with many able men, and not primarily as a representative of her sex. Nevertheless I am sure she will forgive this virtually all-male audience if we find some special inspiration in the fact that besides all of her other accomplishments, she is a very charming woman as well. It is to India's everlasting credit that Mrs. Gandhi has not been hampered by prejudices that still handicap her sex in so many parts of the world. Interestingly enough, equal opportunity for women has certainly not been characteristic of India over the centuries; and it has been only through the efforts of leaders such as Mr. Nehru and Mrs. Gandhi herself that India has advanced to the front rank of nations in this respect.

Ladies and gentlemen, it is with the greatest pleasure that I present to you a person of talent, charm and dignity, a many-faceted human being, Her Excellency Indira Gandhi, Prime Minister of India. *[Waits until the end of the speech to give the speaker's name and begin the applause.]*

"Address to the Nation: The *Challenger* Tragedy"
Ronald Reagan

On January 28, 1986, the space shuttle Challenger *exploded shortly after lift-off, killing all seven crew members including a schoolteacher from New Hampshire. Following the disaster, President Reagan delivered this moving address to the American people. This speech falls under the category of "special speeches" that we discussed in Chapter Five. Reagan's main goal was to offer sympathy for the families of the astronauts and give encouragement to the nation.*

Ladies and gentlemen, I'd planned to speak to you tonight to report on the State of the Union. But the events of earlier today have led me to change those plans. Today is a day for mourning and remembering. *[Begins to talk about the loss of the astronauts.]*

Nancy and I are pained to the core by the tragedy of the shuttle, *Challenger.* We know we share this pain with all of the people of our country. This is truly a national loss.

Nineteen years ago, almost to the day, we lost three astronauts in a terrible accident on the ground. But we've never lost an astronaut in flight; we've never had a tragedy like this. And perhaps we've forgotten the courage it took for the crew of the shuttle.

But they, the *Challenger* Seven, were aware of the dangers, but overcame them and did their jobs brilliantly. We mourn seven heroes: Michael Smith, Dick Scobee, Judith Resnik, Ronald McNair, Ellison Onizuka, Gregory Jarvis, and Christa McAuliffe. We mourn their loss as a nation together.

For the families of the seven, we cannot bear, as you do, the full impact of this tragedy. But we feel the loss and we are thinking about you so very much. Your loved ones were daring and brave and they had that special grace, that special spirit that says, "Give me a challenge and I'll meet it with joy." They had a hunger to explore the universe and discover its truths. They wished to serve, and they did. They served all of us.

[Begins to offer encouragement to the nation.] We have grown used to wonders in this century. It's hard to dazzle us. But for 25 years the United States space program has been doing just that. We've grown used to the idea of space, and perhaps we forget that we've only just begun. We're still pioneers. They, the members of the *Challenger* crew, were pioneers.

And I want to say something to the schoolchildren of American who were watching the live coverage of the shuttle's take-off. I know it is hard to understand, but sometimes painful things like this happen. It's all a part of the process of exploration and discovery. It's all part of taking a chance and expanding man's horizons. The future doesn't belong to the fainthearted. It belongs to the brave. The *Challenger* crew was pulling us into the future, and we'll continue to follow them.

I've always had great faith in and respect for our space program, and what happened today does nothing to diminish it. We don't hide our space program. We don't keep secrets and cover things up. We do it all up front and in public. That's the way freedom is, and we wouldn't change it for one minute.

We'll continue our quest in space. There will be more shuttle flights and more shuttle crews and, yes, more volunteers, more civilians, more teachers in space. Nothing ends here. Our hopes and our journeys continue.

I want to add that I wish I could talk to every man and women who works for NASA or who worked on this mission and tell them, "Your dedication and professionalism have moved and impressed us for decades. And we know of your anguish. We share it."

[Begins conclusion remarks.] There's a coincidence today. On this day 390 years ago, the great explorer, Sir Francis Drake, died aboard ship off the coast of Panama. In his lifetime, the great frontiers were the oceans and a historian later said, "He lived by the sea, died on it and was buried in it." Well, today, we can say of the *Challenger* crew their dedication was, like Drake's, complete.

The crew of the space shuttle *Challenger* honored us by the manner in which they lived their lives. We will never forget them, nor the last time we saw them, this morning, as they prepared for their journey and waved goodbye and "slipped the surly bonds of Earth to touch...the face of God."

Thank you. *[Ends the speech with a quotation from a poem by John Gillespie Magee, Jr., an American pilot who was killed in a plane crash over England in 1941.]*

One Hundred Great Speeches

The following is a chronological list of one hundred famous speeches from c. 2000 B.C. to 1990. Developing this collection was very interesting. In the older works, you'll notice that many of the speakers were eventually executed for boldly stating their religious and political beliefs. Some of them even delivered their speeches moments before their deaths. In the later works, you will see many proclamations of war and encouraging words to soldiers in battle. But I have ended this list of great speeches with an address given by Barbara Bush at Wellesley College's commencement where she shared the speaking event with Raisa Gorbachev, wife of Mikhail Gorbachev. I think this says a lot for the progress of mankind, and I think it is a good way to end a list of great speeches.

The Ancient World

Job: *In Response to the Advice of His Friends.* This speech was delivered c. 2000 B.C. and is probably the oldest recorded speech.

Moses: *Proclamation of The Ten Commandments.* Delivered c. 1406 B.C. to the nation of Israel from Mt. Sinai.

Isaiah: *A Cry for Social Justice.* Delivered c. 720 B.C. to the nation of Israel.

Socrates: *On His Condemnation to Death.* Socrates was sentenced to death for not accepting the gods and for corrupting the Athenian youth. This speech was delivered after his death sentence in 399 B.C.

Isocrates: *On the Union of Greece to Resist Persia.* Isocrates was considered one of the greatest speech writers of the period. This speech was delivered in 380 B.C.

Demosthenes: *Denounces the Imperialistic Ambitions of Philip of Macedon.* A great speaker who often spoke against politicians. This speech was delivered in c. 341 B.C.

Hannibal: *To His Soldiers.* Hannibal was a Carthaginian general who delivered this speech after his army had crossed the Alps and entered Italy, 218 B.C.

Cato: *Demanding the Execution of Conspirators.* Delivered 63 B.C. to the senate in opposition to Caesar's position.

Cicero: *Against Catiline and His Followers.* Delivered to the Roman Senate in December, 63 B.C. encouraging the execution of Catiline who had tried to assassinate him.

Catiline: *Encouraging His Soliders to Fight.* Catiline, the famous Roman politician and general, delivered this speech to his small band of followers after fleeing Rome to escape execution and being cornered at Pistoria. Delivered in January, 62 B.C., he was killed in the battle that followed.

Julius Caesar: *On the Treatment of the Conspirators.* Delivered to the senate c. 60 B.C.

Jesus: *Sermon on the Mount.* His most famous sermon delivered c. 33 A.D.

Peter: *Address to the Crowd on the Day of Pentecost.* Delivered in Jerusalem c. 34 A.D.

Stephen: *Address to the Sanhedrin.* Stephen's famous sermon resulting in his death c. 34 A.D.

Chrysostom: *The Fall of Eutropius, Minister of State.* Delivered in 398 against the mob who wanted Eutropius, a religious reformer, murdered.

Empress Theodora: *Refusing to Flee.* When Emperor Justinian of Rome was almost overthrown by rebels, the Empress Theodora made a brief speech that encouraged their defense and led to the slaughter of the rebels. Delivered January 18, 532.

Bede: *Sermon on the Nativity of St. Peter and St. Paul.* The famous English monk and scholar delivered this sermon c. 715.

Bernard of Clairvaux: *The Name of Jesus.* One of his many sermons delivered in 1136.

The Middle Ages/Renaissance

St. Francis: *Sermon to the Birds.* St. Francis renounced all worldliness and lived a life of self-denial. He preached to all people, and sometimes even animals. Delivered c. 1200.

John Wyclif: *Sixth Sunday After Easter Sermon.* Wyclif was a religious reformer who often denounced the Pope. This sermon was delivered c. 1381.

Girolamo Savonarola: *Addressing the People of Florence about Repentance.* Delivered on the Feast of the Ascension, May 12, 1496.

Hugh Latimer: *Christian Love.* Latimer was one of the Oxford martyrs of the English Reformation period. This is one of his many sermons delivered c. 1515.

Huldreich Zwingli: *Evils of Foreign Military Service.* At the time of this speech, Zwingli's country, Switzerland, was troubled with mercenary warfare. In this speech, c. 1520, he spoke strongly against this evil.

Martin Luther: *Defending Himself at the Diet of Worms.* Delivered to an assembly of nobles on April 18, 1521.

Sir Thomas Moore: *His Defense Against the Charges of Treason.* Thomas Moore was one of Henry VIII's most trusted advisors. When Moore denied Henry's right to be called the "supreme head" of the Church of England, he was convicted of treason. This speech was given a few days before his execution on July 7, 1535.

Thomas Cranmer: *Sermon on Good Works.* Cranmer, an English statesman and philosopher, delivered this sermon c. 1540.

John Calvin: *On Suffering Persecution.* Delivered during the Protestant Reformation c. 1541.

John Knox: *The Temptation of Christ.* Knox was a Scottish reformer and statesman. This is one of his many popular sermons delivered c. 1547.

Peter Wentworth: *Liberties of Parliament.* Wentworth, a famous English parliamentary speaker, delivered this speech to the House of Commons on February 8, 1576.

Queen Elizabeth: *The Armada Peril.* A patriotic, encouraging speech against the Spanish Armada delivered on July 29, 1588.

Sir John Eliot: *Speech on the Petition of Right.* Delivered June 2, 1628, to the House of Commons against the Duke of Buckingham.

John Winthrop: *The Goal of Government Officials.* Delivered in 1630 aboard the *Arella,* as they were sailing for the New World.

John Donne: *His Own Funeral Sermon.* Delivered on the first Friday in Lent, 1631. Donne was seriously ill and many of the audience members commented that he seemed to be delivering his own funeral sermon.

John Pym: *Speech Against Strafford.* Pym, a Puritan statesman and parliamentary leader, delivered this speech to the lords in Parliament on April 12, 1641, against the Earl of Strafford who was charged with treason.

Oliver Cromwell: *Speech at the Opening of the First Protective Parliament.* Delivered September 4, 1654, in England.

Thomas Harrison: *On His Death Sentence.* Delivered to the crowd after he, along with 26 advocates of Charles I's execution, was sentenced to death on October 13, 1660.

Richard Rumbold: *On His Death Sentence.* Delivered in June 1685. Rumbold was one of the Puritan leaders who was executed following the restoration of the Stuart monarchy.

The Age of Enlightenment

Jean Massillon: *The Curse of a Malignant Tongue.* Massillon was a French religious reformer and orator who delivered this sermon c. 1715.

John Wesley: *The Free Grace of God.* Delivered in 1739 near Bristol against the doctrine of predestination.

William Pitt: *Taxation Without Representation.* Delivered to the House of Commons on January 14, 1766.

Patrick Henry: *American Revolution Speech.* Delivered in Richmond, Virginia, on March 28, 1775.

George Washington: *Talking His Officers Out of Insurrection.* Delivered on March 15, 1783, at Newburgh, New York, encouraging the war effort to continue.

Benjamin Franklin: *Closing the Constitutional Convention.* Delivered on September 17, 1787.

Mirabeau: *The King's Right To Make War and Peace.* Delivered on May 22, 1790, in favor of the King of Spain.

James Otis: *Illegal Search and Seizure.* Delivered on February 24, 1791, against illegal search and seizure. This speech contains several commonly quoted phrases such as "a man's house is his castle...."

Georges Jacques Danton: *To Dare Again....* Danton was one of the greatest speakers of the French Revolution. This speech was delivered to the National Assembly in 1792.

Camille Desmoulins: *Advocating the Execution of Louis XVI.* Desmoulins was a very violent political speaker. This speech was delivered at the National Convention in 1793.

Seth Luther: *Address to New England Workingmen.* Delivered c. 1832 in several cities against the New England labor system.

Frederick Douglass: *Speech at Music Hall, Boston.* Born as a slave, Douglass educated himself and became a popular speaker. This speech was delivered in 1841 at one of the many "free speech" meetings in Boston.

Elizabeth Caddy Stanton: *Keynote at the First Women's Rights Convention.* Delivered on July 19, 1848, at Seneca Falls, New York.

Jefferson Davis: *North and South Relations.* The President of the Southern Confederacy delivered this speech on February 4, 1850.

Thaddeus Stevens: *Fanaticism and Liberty.* One of his many speeches against slavery and against the Compromise of 1850. Delivered c. 1850.

Louis Pasteur: *Spirit and Science.* Delivered on December 7, 1854, at the University of Strasbourg.

Abraham Lincoln: *The Gettysburg Address.* Delivered on November 19, 1863, in Gettysburg, Pennsylvania.

Charles Dickens: *English Friendship for America.* A farewell address given at a dinner in his honor in New York City, April 18, 1868.

Susan B. Anthony: *Women's Right to Suffrage.* Delivered in 1872 after her arrest for voting.

Francis Williard: *Safeguards for Women.* Delivered in 1876 in Philadelphia on women's right to vote.

John Daniel: *Dedication of the Washington Monument.* Delivered on February 21, 1885, to the U.S. House of Representatives.

Belva A. Lockwood: *Political Rights of Women.* Delivered c. 1885 to a Congressional Committee about women's suffrage.

Booker T. Washington: *The Heroes of Fort Wagner.* Delivered on May 31 ,1897, in Boston.

Horace Porter: *The Life of Lincoln.* Delivered to the Republican Club of New York City on the 90 anniversary of the birth of Lincoln, February 12, 1889.

Joseph Jefferson: *My Farm.* A humorous speech delivered to the Author's Club in New York City, February 28, 1893.

William Jennings Bryan: *America's Mission.* Delivered on February 22, 1899, in Washington, D.C. to the Washington Day Banquet given by the Virginia Democratic Association.

Mark Twain: *Fourth of July Speech.* Delivered July 4, 1899, at a dinner given by the American Society.

Modern Times

F. Charles Hume: *The Young Lawyer.* Delivered on August 31, 1906, at a dinner for the American Bar Association in Minneapolis.

William Howard Taft: *The President.* Delivered on November 16, 1912, at a dinner at the Lotos Club in New York City.

Cardinal Desire Mercier: *A Sermon in German Occupied Brussels.* Delivered in the Cathedral of Brussels on July 21, 1916.

Woodrow Wilson: *Peace Without Victory.* Delivered to the Senate on January 21, 1917.

Woodrow Wilson: *Asking Congress to Declare War Against Germany.* Delivered on April 2, 1917.

Wendell Phillips Stafford: *The College: A Training School for Public Service.* Delivered on October 20, 1919, at Dartmouth College.

Will Rogers: *Wealth and Education.* This is one of the few recorded humorous speeches of Rogers, delivered at a dinner given by the alumni of Columbia University in New York City, December 4, 1924.

Franklin D. Roosevelt: *Inaugural Address.* Delivered on March 4, 1933.

Franklin D. Roosevelt: *Bank Closings.* The first of Roosevelt's Fireside Chats. Radio broadcast on March 12, 1933.

William Lyon Phelps: *Owning Books.* A radio address delivered on April 6, 1933.

Winston Churchhill: *This Was Their Finest Hour.* Delivered in June 18, 1940, in England.

Franklin D. Roosevelt: *Declaration of War.* Delivered to Congress on December 8, 1941, after the Japanese attack on Pearl Harbor.

John D. Rockefeller, Jr.: *Our Family Creed.* A radio broadcast delivered on July 8, 1941.

David Lilienthal: *A Definition of Democracy.* Delivered to the Joint Congressional Committee on Atomic Energy after a fierce attack on his nomination to become the new head of the atomic energy program. After this speech given on February 3, 1947, Lilienthal got the job.

Jawaharlal Nehru: *Speaking to Mourners a Few Hours After the Murder of Gandhi.* Delivered on January 30, 1948.

Albert Einstein: *In Memory of Max Planck.* Delivered at a 1948 memorial service for Max Planck, the father of the theory of quantum mechanics.

Harry S. Truman: *Inaugural Address.* Delivered on January 20, 1949.

William Faulkner: *Nobel Prize Speech.* Delivered on December 10, 1950, in Stockholm, Sweden.

Douglas MacArthur: *In Defense of His Conduct in the Korean War.* Delivered April 19, 1951, to both Houses of Congress, which was unheard of in American history.

Dwight D. Eisenhower: *Inaugural Address.* Delivered on January 20, 1953.

Carl Sandburg: *Address on the Anniversary of Lincoln's Birth.* Delivered on February 12, 1959, to Congress.

John F. Kennedy: *Inaugural Address.* Delivered on January 20, 1961, in Washington, D.C.

Douglas MacArthur: *Duty, Honor, and Country.* Delivered to the West Point Cadets on May 12, 1962.

Martin Luther King, Jr.: *I Have a Dream.* Delivered on August 28, 1963, in Washington, D.C.

Lyndon B. Johnson: *Opportunity for Education.* Delivered January 12, 1965, to Congress. This speech is often considered the most comprehensive proposal ever made for education.

Alfred Hayes: *Speech Introducing Indira Gandhi.* Delivered in 1966 to the Economic Club of New York, introducing the Prime Minister of India.

Barbara Jordan: *Keynote Address at the Democratic National Convention.* Delivered on July 12, 1976, in New York City.

Art Buchwald: *Address to Graduates.* Delivered on May 7, 1977, to the graduating class of Catholic University's Columbus School of Law in Washington, D.C.

Rosalyn Yalow: *Join Hands, Hearts, and Minds.* In acceptance of the Nobel Prize. Delivered in 1977 in Stockholm, Sweden.

A.M. Rosenthal: *Freedom of the Press.* Rosenthal, of the *New York Times,* delivered this speech at Colby College in Waterville, Maine, on November 18, 1981.

Carl Sagan: *1984 and 2001: A New Year's Resolution.* Delivered on December 31, 1983, in New York City.

Billy Graham: *Salvation.* Delivered on September 18, 1984, in Novosibirsk, Siberia.

Ronald Reagan: *Address to the Nation: The* Challenger *Tragedy.* Televised on January 28, 1986, from Washington, D.C.

Gerry Sikorski: *Will and Vision, The Tools You Need.* Commencement address delivered on June 1, 1986, in Breckenridge, Minnesota.

Ted Koppel: *The Newsworthiness of the Ten Commandments.* Delivered on May 10, 1987, to the graduating class at Duke University.

Barbara Bush: *Commencement Address at Wellesley College.* Delivered at Wellesley College, Massachusetts, June 1, 1990. At this event, Mrs. Bush "shared the podium" with Raisa Gorbachev.

For Further Information

As you write your speeches, you will discover that you need resources to help you find useful quotes, stories, jokes, examples, and other information that make a speech effective and interesting. The following books are all very good and will give you many ideas.

Adams, Ramon. *The Cowboy Dictionary*. New York, NY: Putnam, 1993.

Applewhite, Ashton. *And I Quote*. New York, NY: St. Martin's Press, 1992.

Buescher, Walter. *Walt Buescher's Library of Humor*. Englewood Cliffs, NJ: Prentice-Hall, 1984.

Byrne, Robert. *911 Best Things Anybody Ever Said*. New York, NY: Random House, 1988.

Canfield, Jack, and Mark Victor Hansen. *Chicken Soup for the Soul*. Deerfield Beach, FL: Health Communications, Inc., 1993.

Canfield, Jack, and Mark Victor Hansen. *A 2nd Helping of Chicken Soup for the Soul*. Deerfield Beach, FL: Health Communications, Inc., 1995.

Claro, Joe. *Jokes & Anecdotes*. New York, NY: Random House, 1994.

Dickson, Paul. *Toasts*. New York, NY: Crown Publishers, 1991.

Doan, Eleanor. *Speaker's Sourcebook*. Grand Rapids, MI: Zondervan, 1988.

Fulghum, Robert. *All I Really Needed to Know I Learned in Kindergarten*. New York, NY: Ballantine Books, 1988.

Fulghum, Robert. *Uh-Oh. Some Observations From Both Sides of the Refrigerator Door.* New York, NY: Ballantine Books, 1991.

Funk, Charles. *Heavens to Betsy and Other Curious Sayings.* New York, NY: Harper & Row, 1983.

Griffin, Jack. *How To Say It Best.* Englewood Cliffs, NJ: Prentice-Hall, 1994.

Henry, Lewis C. *Best Quotations for All Occasions.* New York, NY: Doubleday, 1993.

Iapoce, Michael. *A Funny Thing Happened on the Way to the Boardroom: Using Humor in Business Speaking.* New York, NY: Wiley, 1988.

Kipfer, Barbara Ann. *14,000 Things To Be Happy About.* New York, NY: Workman Publishing, 1990.

Kipfer, Barbara Ann. *Bartlett's Book of Business Quotations.* New York, NY: Little, Brown, 1994.

Lieberman, Gerald. *3,500 Quotes for Speakers.* New York, NY: Doubleday, 1983.

Miller, J.R. *The 901 Best Jokes There Ever Was.* Nashville, TN: Rutledge Hill Press, 1991.

Miner, Margaret, and Hugh Rawson. *The New International Dictionary of Quotations.* New York, NY: Penguin Books, 1993.

Miner, Margaret, and Hugh Rawson. *A Dictionary of Quotations from Shakespeare.* New York, NY: Penguin Books, 1994.

Manchak, Susan. *Encyclopedia of School Humor.* West Nyack, NY: Parker Publishing Co., 1987.

Orben, Robert. *2400 Jokes To Brighten Your Speeches.* New York, NY: Doubleday, 1984.

Partington, Angela. *The Concise Oxford Dictionary of Quotations.* New York, NY: Oxford University Press, 1994.

Pasta, Elmer. *Complete Book of Roasts, Boasts, and Toasts.* West Nyack, NY: Parker Publishing Co., 1982.

Pendleton, Winston. *Speaker's Handbook of Successful Openers and Closers.* Englewood Cliffs, NJ: Prentice-Hall, 1984.

Prochnow, Herbert. *The Toastmaster's Treasure Chest.* New York, NY: Harper & Row, 1988.

Rovin, Jeff. *1,001 More Great Jokes.* New York, NY: Penguin Books, 1989.

Rovin, Jeff. *1,001 Great Sports Jokes.* New York, NY: Penguin Books, 1991.

Rovin, Jeff. *500 Great Lawyer Jokes.* New York, NY: Penguin Books, 1992.

Rovin, Jeff. 500 Great Doctor Jokes. New York, NY: Penguin Books, 1993.

Spinrad, Leonard. *Complete Speaker's Almanac.* Englewood Cliffs, NJ: Prentice-Hall, 1984.

Tomlinson, Gerald. *Speaker's Treasury of Sports Anecdotes, Stories, and Humor.* Englewood Cliffs, NJ: Prentice-Hall, 1990.

Walters, Lilly. *What To Say When You're Dying on the Platform.* New York, NY: McGraw-Hill, 1995.

Wollard, Kathy. *How Come?* New York, NY: Workman Publishing Co., 1993.

Wright, John. *The Universal Almanac 1995.* Kansas City, MO: Andrews & McNeel, 1995.

Youngman, *Henry. 10,000 One Liners.* Katonah, NY: Ballymote Books, 1989.

Public Speaking/Presentation Books

From time to time, you may realize that you need specific information about a certain type of public speaking, presentation, or even performance problem. The following books about public speaking and presentations are more specialized and focus on certain topics.

Anderson, James. *Speaking to Groups: Eyeball to Eyeball.* Vienna, VA: Wyndmoor Press, 1989.

Axtell, Roger. *The Do's and Taboos of Public Speaking: How To Get Those Butterflies To Fly in Formation.* New York, NY: Wiley, 1992.

Booher, Dianna. *Executive's Portfolio of Model Speeches for All Occasions.* Englewood Cliffs, NJ: Prentice-Hall, 1993.

Bower, Sharon. *Painless Public Speaking.* Englewood Cliffs, NJ: Prentice-Hall, 1981.

Buys, William. *Creative Speaking.* Lincolnwood, IL: National Textbook Co., 1989.

Carnegie, Dale. *The Quick & Easy Way to Effective Speaking.* New York, NY: Simon & Schuster, 1962.

Detz, Joan. *How To Write and Give a Speech.* New York, NY: St. Martin's Press, 1992.

Echeverria, Ellen. *Speaking on Issues.* New York, NY: Holt, Rinehart, and Winston, 1987.

Elgin, Suzette. *BusinessSpeak: Using the Gentle Art of Verbal Persuasion To Get What You Want at Work.* New York, NY: McGraw-Hill, 1995.

Fletcher, Leon. *How To Speak Like a Pro.* New York, NY: Random House, 1983.

Gard, Grant. *The Art of Confident Speaking.* Englewood Cliffs, NJ: Prentice-Hall, 1986.

Hilton, Jack. *How To Meet the Press: A Survival Guide.* Champaign, IL: Sagamore Publishing, 1990.

Kayfetz, Janet. *Academically Speaking.* Belmont, CA: Wadsworth Publishing, 1987.

Koch, Arthur. *Speaking with a Purpose.* Englewood Cliffs, NJ: Prentice-Hall, 1988.

Koehler, Jerry. *Public Communication in Business and the Professions.* St. Paul, MN: West Publishing Co., 1981.

Lambert, Clark. *The Business Presentations Workbook.* Englewood Cliffs, NJ: Prentice-Hall, 1989.

Linver, Sandy. *Speak and Get Results.* New York, NY: Summit Books, 1983.

Mandel, Steve. *Effective Presentation Skills.* Los Altos, CA: Crisp Publications, 1987.

Modisett, Noah, and James Luter, Jr. *Speaking Clearly. The Basics of Voice and Articulation.* Edina, MN: Burgess International Group, 1988.

Nelson, Paul. *Confidence in Public Speaking.* Dubuque, IA: W.C. Brown, 1981.

Nelson, Robert. *The Presentation Primer: Getting Your Point Across.* Burr Ridge, IL: Irwin Professional, 1994.

Packham, Jo. *Wedding Toasts & Speeches.* New York, NY: Sterling Publishing Co., 1993.

Paulson, Lynda. *The Executive Persuader.* Napa, CA: R&E Publishers, 1991.

Rafe, Stephen. *How To Be Prepared To Think on Your Feet.* New York, NY: Harper Business, 1990.

Sarnoff, Dorothy. *Never Be Nervous Again.* New York, NY: Crown Publishers, 1987.

Shea, Gordon. *Managing a Difficult or Hostile Audience.* Englewood Cliffs, NJ: Prentice-Hall, 1984.

Smith, Terry. *Making Successful Presentations: A Self-Teaching Guide.* New York, NY: Wiley, 1991.

Sprague, Jo, and Douglas Stuart. *The Speaker's Handbook.* New York, NY: Harcourt Brace Jovanovich, 1984.

Thomsett, Michael. *The Little Black Book of Business Speaking.* New York, NY: American Press, 1989.

Turner, William. *Secrets of Persuasion.* Englewood Cliffs, NJ: Prentice-Hall, 1985.

Vasile, Albert. *Speak with Confidence: A Practical Guide.* New York, NY: Little, Brown, 1986.

Walters, Dottie. *Speak and Grow Rich.* Englewood Cliffs, NJ: Prentice-Hall, 1989.

Wilder, Lilyan. *Professionally Speaking: Getting Ahead in Business.* New York, NY: Simon & Schuster, 1986.

Youga, Janet. *The Elements of Audience Analysis.* New York, NY: Macmillan, 1989.

The Study of Communication

If you are interested in learning more about communication, the following books are all very informative, yet easy to use and understand.

Argyle, Michael. *Bodily Communication.* New York, NY: Methuen Press, 1988.

Brooks, William D. *Speech Communication.* Dubuque, IA: W.C. Brown, 1985.

DeVito, Joseph A. *Human Communication.* New York, NY: Harper & Row, 1988.

Gronbeck, Bruce. *Principles of Speech Communication.* New York, NY: Harper-Collins, 1992.

Knapp, Mark. *Nonverbal Communication in Human Interaction.* New York, NY: Holt, Rinehart, and Winston, 1972.

Larson, Charles. *Persuasion, Perception, and Responsibility.* Belmont, CA: Wadsworth Publishing Co., 1989.

Osborn, Michael, and Suzanne Osborn. *Public Speaking.* Boston, MA: Houghton Mifflin Company, 1988.

Poyatos, Fernando. *New Perspectives in Nonverbal Communication.* New York, NY: Pergamon Press, 1983.

Verderber, Rudolph F. *The Challenge of Effective Speaking.* Belmont, CA: Wadsworth Publishing, 1988.

Audiovisual Products

As you work to develop your public speaking skills, you may need some audiovisual materials to help you improve your performance. I have listed several quality products and the companies you should contact for ordering information.

**Available from
Toastmaster's International,
P.O. Box 10400, Santa Ana, CA 92711:**

Be Prepared To Speak. Video that examines speech writing, presentation skills, and stage fright.

Humor, Speaking, and You! Four audio cassettes about how to use humor in your speeches. Includes many examples.
The Effective Speaker. Six audio cassettes that discuss the qualities of an effective speaker. Many famous examples are included.

Communicate What You Think. Six-audio cassette programs on speaking, listening, organizing, and persuading.

The Compleat Speaker. Six audio cassettes discuss a wide variety of public speaking issues.

**Available from
Walters Speaker Services,
P.O. Box 1120, Glendora, CA 91740:**

How To Enter the World of Paid Public Speaking. Six-audio cassette album.

Persuasive Platform Presentations: Secrets of Successful Speakers. Four audio cassettes and workbook.

Games Presenters Play. Video of ice-breakers and audience activities.

How To Create & Market Speaker Products. Six audio cassette album.

If you are interested in great public speakers of the past, try the following speech collections:

Great American Speeches (audio tape). New York, NY: Caedmon, 1968.

Great Black Speeches (audio tape). New York, NY: HarperCollins, 1974.

Great American Women's Speeches (audio tape). New York, NY: Caedmon, 1973.

The Inaugural Address of John F. Kennedy (audio tape). New York, NY: Spoken Arts, 1969.

Roehling, Edward. *Great Speeches* (video tape). Greenwood, IL: Alliance Video Corp., 1985.

Computer Software

With the explosion of the computer software market in the past several years, a number of quality programs are available for Macintosh and IBM compatible computers that are beneficial for public speakers.

Adobe Persuasion 3.0. This presentation program will help you to generate various media products that can be used in public speaking. *Broderbund Print Shop Deluxe.* This application creates calendars, cards, posters, and other products. It is especially useful for lettering and graphics on your visual aids.

ClarisWorks 4.0. This all-in-one application contains word-processing, spreadsheet, database, presentation, draw/paint, and communications capabilities.

Famous American Speeches: A Multimedia History – 1850 to the Present. Includes text and video footage for more than 300 speeches. Available from Oryx

Gold Disk Astound 2.0. This multimedia program can create effective slides, handouts, and "on-screen" visual aids.

Microsoft PowerPoint 4.0. This is a presentation program that creates media products and even helps you practice your presentation! You can create presentations very quickly with this application, and I believe it is a "must have" for the serious public speaker.

Photodisk ClipPix. CD-ROM for Mac or Windows that contains over 500 photographs that can be used on your visual aids.

Index